# REAL ESTATE INVESTING FOR EVERYONE

## A Guide to Creating Financial Freedom

## Martin Stone

### ixia
PRESS

Mineola, New York

*Bibliographical Note*

*Real Estate Investing for Everyone: A Guide to Creating Financial Freedom*
is a new work, first published by Ixia Press in 2019.

*Library of Congress Cataloging-in-Publication Data*

Names: Stone, Martin, 1948– author.
Title: Real estate investing for everyone : a guide to creating financial
    freedom / Martin Stone.
Description: Mineola : Ixia Press, 2019.
Identifiers: LCCN 2018024179 | ISBN 9780486820859 (paperback) |
    ISBN 0486820858
Subjects: LCSH: Real estate investment. | Investments.
Classification: LCC HD1382.5 .S758 2019 | DDC 332.63/24—dc23
LC record available at https://lccn.loc.gov/2018024179

Ixia Press
An imprint of Dover Publications, Inc.

Manufactured in the United States by LSC Communications
82085801    2019
www.doverpublications.com/ixiapress

# Contents

# Introduction

A simple Internet search uncovers more than thirteen thousand books available on the topic of real estate investing. Regrettably missing from the lion's share of those books are chapters devoted to discussing the *reasons* to invest—that is, recognizing what the true and long-term financial benefits are to owning income property and then, most important, learning how to use those benefits to fund the kind of life and, ultimately, the kind of retirement you truly desire. Our plan here is to tackle this missing piece of the real estate investing puzzle head-on.

The birth of this book came about from lessons learned in my everyday business as a real estate broker, selling investment property to people like you for more than forty years. The lessons I'm going to share with you here are the same ones my colleagues and I have been preaching to our own clients for all these years. These lessons have helped to create wealth and stability for them, and they can do the same for you too.

Visit any online source or walk into any bookstore and you will see shelves full of titles promising to make you wealthy using this or that system. In fact, lots of books offer sound advice on how to build wealth in many arenas, not just real estate. *We concluded that the problem is most books on this subject are offering a road map to riches to people who aren't committed to the trip.*

For many busy working people, saving money and thinking about setting up a plan is the last thing they want to consider. They are pulling in a decent paycheck every week, spending it on bills and pleasure, and because they are young and energetic, they are confident they can keep that train running for as long as necessary. Hopefully, something kicks in—let's call it "maturity"—and they realize what a dead-end merry-go-round they are on. Now, investing a portion of their salary toward a fruitful future becomes a top priority. Better late than never, right? With clients like this, we no longer talk about retirement planning. We focus on investing to find the financial freedom to live their life the way they want to live it.

Statistics show that for almost 95 percent of all retirees, there is no golf club membership, no exciting vacations to be had and, literally, no rest for the weary. Sadly, the blessing of abundance in our country has created a generation of people who believe everything is going to work out just fine in the end. The sad truth is it is not.

Many people spend a good deal of time planning the profitability of the companies they work for yet do nothing to create the same kind of security for their own families. Often it is not until they get the boot because of company cutbacks that they realize it is too late. Or, worse yet, they do not wake up until after they get a gold watch and a round of "For He's a Jolly Good Fellow."

Everyone has read about the golden parachutes that top executives get when they leave major companies. Those executives plan for those parachutes when they start their jobs. In fact, without a guarantee of one on the way out, they refuse to take the position. Now check with the human resources department where you're working. Did anyone create a golden parachute to help protect you when your tenure is over? Of course not!

The truth is, there is probably the equivalent of a teeny, tiny umbrella set aside for you, if there is anything at all. Two weeks of severance pay for years of service is hardly what anyone would call "golden." And you will get an even smaller umbrella from Social Security. This is not very comforting after a lifetime of paying into the system!

My plan in this book is to show you how to create your own golden parachute via investments in real estate. It can be done. I've done it for myself and have helped countless others do it for themselves too.

I will educate you in the same conservative investment techniques that I have espoused to my clients for the past forty years. Here, I will teach you that success in real estate does not take smoke, does not include mirrors, and does not require luck. Rather, success here simply requires a well-thought-out road map. The good news is the nucleus of your road map is now resting in your hands.

Thomas Jefferson said, "Most people believe that they'll wake up some day and find themselves rich." Jefferson got it only half-right. Eventually people do wake up. Unfortunately, when they do, it is usually too late. My hope is you grab the ideas in this book, couple them with your own dreams and actions, and make something fantastic happen for yourself.

"Why real estate?" you ask. Don't most people invest in the stock market or mutual funds? The answer to that is *yes*. I disagree that it is a good strategy, but more about that in a later section. The reason I believe in real estate so strongly is it is a basic necessity of life, the others being food, clothing, and shelter. Everyone needs these basics, so by investing in real estate you are banking on something that people will *always* need. The food and clothing industries do not lend themselves well to passive financing, but the real estate industry does. When I say "passive investing," I mean that you can outsource most, if not all, of the work necessary to manage one of these investments.

For the purposes of this guide I am not talking about single-family houses but about rental property. In most metropolitan areas there is a definite need for rental housing for all the people who cannot afford to buy their own homes. It's no secret that in those same areas the population grows every year as families add more children, people move in from other areas, and older housing is removed to make room for new housing.

Along with all this demand, most cities, counties, and states are making it tougher every year to build new housing. The codes are getting tougher, the zoning is getting more restrictive, and the costs are increasing at all levels. So, we see a growing demand for housing and less and less construction. All this drives up the cost to buy and to rent. This sounds bad, unless you are in the business of owning a basic commodity that everyone needs and one where competition is slowing down because government is making it tougher to build.

I have made a point of urging my clients to get more involved in managing their own affairs. I advise you to do the same: at least put as much effort into that as you put into your career (where you trade your time for dollars you make to pay the bills). I also understand that, despite all the advances in life, we are busier than ever, so time is precious to us.

I personally own several properties that were built prior to the Great Depression, and they are giving me a great return. I have visited San Francisco frequently, and most of those classic Victorian and Edwardian homes also are from that same era and sell for a huge amount today. My point here is simple: yes, real estate does go through cycles, and you have to be financially prepared for them. We do get through these rough times and things improve, but unlike most businesses, property does not lose its ability to provide housing and therefore consistently provides a return on investment.

The key thing that helps real estate perform so well is the land. As you know, there are millions of acres in the United States and there is nothing on them, so they are virtually worthless. If you look in most major cities, it is just the opposite; there is little or no vacant land. It is actually the value of the land that helps real estate perform favorably. It's not the structures on top of the land. Older homes are torn down to build newer, larger homes. Antiquated apartment buildings are demolished to build condominiums. The reason is the land alone has become more valuable than the land with the aged structure on it. It is this irreplaceable component of real estate investment that almost guarantees your continuing return.

Several years back I decided to take a hard look at what a career really does to one's life. Somewhere I had read a very simple statement: "Your work isn't your life." I can't tell you what it is that makes us happy, but my guess is that as much as we might like what we do to earn a living, it is still work. Where I come from, they have a saying: "The worst day fishing is better than the best day working." So I decided to have a look at comparing work with vacation, believing that most people do things they really like to do when they get a break. To create this chart, I assumed most people get two weeks of vacation a year and work five days a week for half the year and six days for the balance. I have no doubt that the way the job market is today, most successful people probably work more than eight hours a day and may even skip vacation or save days off for later. Below are a blank chart and an example.

## WORK VERSUS VACATION UNTIL RETIREMENT AT 65

$$\frac{\qquad}{A} \times 275 = \underline{\qquad} \quad \text{Work Days Left}$$

$$\frac{\qquad}{A} \times 14 = \underline{\qquad} \quad \text{Vacation Days until 65}$$

A = Subtract Your Current Age from 65

Assume You Are 30

$$35 \times 275 = 9,625 \quad \text{Days of Work Left}$$

$$35 \times 14 = 490 \quad \text{Vacation Days}$$

Experience can be a great teacher because it gives you many examples of good and bad decisions, so I hope you won't repeat the bad decisions. Now when I look back on my life, I am reminded that some of the simplest things I did way back when have had a tremendous impact on my life today. To illustrate what I mean, I imagined how a person's life might be different today at sixty-five years old based upon several choices that they might have made when they started working in 1977.

If this person had not done any investing for retirement, they would be entitled to $2,687 per month from Social Security. The reality is a tremendous number of people in our country never get beyond depending upon Social Security. So after working forty years, which is about ten thousand business days, $2,687 is all the person can expect as a maximum benefit.

Most retirement programs recommend putting away money every month in a savings account. The chart below will give you a couple of examples of what that might do over a forty-year career, assuming you can earn 5 percent on those deposits.

If you want to see how this works, use this online calculator that shows the growth of a constant amount over time. The interest rate can be adjusted. https://www.thecalculatorsite.com/finance/calculators/compoundinterestcalculator.php

| | | |
|---|---|---|
| $100 per month for 40 years | = $153,973 | Actual cash invested $ 48,000 |
| $200 per month for 40 years | = $307,211 | Actual cash invested $ 96,000 |
| $300 per month for 40 years | = $460,449 | Actual cash invested $144,000 |

So that you can compare a real estate investment to the savings account deposit examples above, here is how a typical real estate investment would work. In Hawthorne, California, in 1977, you could have bought a four-unit building for $89,500 with a down payment of $3,200 from an FHA (Federal Housing Administration) loan. Or if you were a veteran, there would have been no down payment required. Today, a similar property is worth $875,000. With the current rents and covering all the expenses, that property would give you $4,150 per month cash flow. In addition, this property would have been paid off ten years before you retired, so in the last ten years it would have produced over $300,000 in positive cash flow.

## MY STORY

I remember the day I realized how being poor felt . . . like it was yesterday. I went to the grocery store for my mom when she was ill. We were on welfare and had to buy items with food stamps, and I recall thinking *What if some of my friends see me buying stuff with food stamps? What will they think?* I ended up walking through the entire store, to make sure the coast was clear, before I put anything in a cart. And then before I proceeded to checkout, I went through the store again to be certain anyone I knew would not see me paying with food stamps. From that day on, my focus was on changing my life so I never would have to feel like that again.

After I came to the realization that I was poor, my early life did not go that well for me. In retrospect, I probably made a bigger deal out of it than anyone else did and I became more conscious of what I didn't have than what I did have. I spent the better part of my early life trying to figure out the quickest way I could change all this, so that I didn't have to worry anymore about something as simple as buying groceries.

I vividly remember discussing careers in high school, civics class. We had a box of cards illustrating different careers, what they were like, how to get there, and the approximate salaries. While some students were looking at jobs they thought they would enjoy, I went through the entire box to find the positions that paid the most. There ended up being a couple that were about the same, so I picked financial services because it also sounded like a pretty classy job to have. I pictured myself working in a bank or a stock brokerage, which seemed great. Shaking the stigma of being a welfare kid was my number one goal in life.

A few years later when I graduated from high school, a couple of friends and I decided to take a trip to Southern California. It was just what we needed to do before we started college. That excursion turned out to be one of the best things I ever did.

I got to visit all the relatives who lived there and spent some time checking out the educational options that were available to me. I was amazed to learn that education in California was almost free versus the high cost of college in Minnesota. Given my background, the choice seemed simple: move to sunny California and go to school for almost nothing! The day I got back to Duluth, I told my mother I was set on heading West to start a new life. She told me that she never liked the cold weather and decided that she and my three younger siblings were heading out there too. We packed everyone up and headed West, where we eventually settled in Lawndale, California.

Once we were moved in, I registered for classes at El Camino College and was excited to get moving on my financial services career path. The reality of our situation hit right away because not only did I have to go to school full-time, but I also had to work full-time to help pay the bills because my two sisters and one brother were still in school. As I would find out later, working provided one of the best opportunities that I've had in my life. At the time, I had no friends in California, but no sooner did I get my first job at Der Wienerschnitzel selling hot dogs than I met my first friend, Bob. We hit it off right away and remain great friends to this day.

Bob's father was a real estate investor and a client of a guy named Jack Buckingham, who started Buckingham Investments. As Bob and I worked our way through college, his father told us about how he was going to retire early from Hughes Aircraft, build a home in the Santa Cruz Mountains, and start his very own vineyard. Bob's dad would come home from work and always complain about how stressful his job as an engineering manager was, and about his desire to get out early so he could enjoy life the way he wanted to. At this point in my life, I had not even started my career, but retiring at an early age sounded great to me. Bob and I always talked about how we were going to become "superbusinessmen" and invest like his father so that we, too, could get out early and enjoy life without restrictions.

After graduating from El Camino, I was fortunate to get a scholarship to attend the University of Southern California, which had a great reputation of helping graduates find successful careers in the world of finance and business. As luck would have it, I graduated right in the middle of the recession of the early 1970s, so despite my finance degree with honors, I could not find a job. For a while, I was paid as a research associate for the State of California, I continued looking for a job and collected unemployment. But all of that soon ran out. Eventually I concluded that since I couldn't find a job in finance, I should consider getting into the real estate business to get a jump on my goal of being an investor like Bob's dad.

Bob, who was also at USC, found himself in the same boat as I was. His dad got ahold of his real estate investment broker, Buckingham, and was able to talk him into taking us under his wing. At the time, this wasn't what I was looking for at all, but I took the chance and gave it the best I had. This decision proved to be far better than any career I could have found. My story is not the skyrocket ride to the good life. I like the saying, "Experience is a great teacher, but you need to use up a lot of your life to get it." I hope that what I share about my experiences in life and in real estate will save you a little of the pain that goes along with living. I firmly believe if I had not taken the chance to become a real estate agent and investor, I would not be close to where I am today financially. As you will learn from my story, it's my belief that financial success means having enough passive income so that one can have the freedom to live their life doing the things with their family that bring the most joy. I hope I can help you get started in your journey to financial success.

So here I am . . . financial services officer turned real estate agent. A strange turn for me, as I never saw myself as a back-slapping, glad-handing salesperson at all. Luckily, my finance background made me curious to how these apartment buildings made money, so I threw myself into the numbers and began to try to understand everything there was about real estate investing. Fortunately, I had a great teacher, Jack Buckingham, who began his career with a degree in physics and went to work in aerospace writing programs to launch and track missiles and satellites. For him this stuff was a walk in the park, and he was an excellent teacher and data-managing fanatic.

One of my first lessons from Jack was I needed to have an investment plan. To me, this sounded bizarre because I didn't have any money to invest. When I told him that, he said, "That's exactly why you need a plan, so you know how you are going to get the money; once you do, you'll know exactly what you are going to do with it!" It took me almost two years of working at Buckingham Investments until I finally created that plan (see figure at end of this section). I took my whole savings and all the money I had stashed under the bed and behind the couch, and I added it up. My first investment plan started with $6,700, and I was determined to put that money to work for me.

During the early years of my real estate career, I basically chased earning more and more money and creating net worth as opposed to making a happy and fulfilling life. "Life is what happens when you are making other plans," and I was on a collision course with this saying. I got married, had a son, and then got divorced. During those same years, our real estate business also hit the skids as we experienced another recession like the one that was in full bloom when I graduated from college. I pulled through and became a better person for it, but it took a lot of dedication and hard work, just like anything in life that is worth having.

I was fortunate to remarry and start a new family, but I found out that having a family and a business and chasing the almighty dollar were big responsibilities and took a lot of time. After weathering another recession, we thought we had everything under control when we found out my wife had breast cancer. Just when I thought I had gotten life on track, it seemed like it was all about to fall apart in a completely different way.

It was now that I learned the value of two things, which I want to share with you. The first was how planning can help in ways that I had not thought of previously. Because of the way I had structured our financial life, I could take time off work and help my wife through the grueling process to beat her cancer. The second lesson was I finally understood something about being rich that Jack always had talked about. When people would speak to him about being rich, he would say, "A rich man is one who knows when he has enough." I had created a plan to make a ton of money, but I had never tied it to a specific goal, which was a huge mistake. What good is a lot of money? How had I spent the last few years with my wife and my kids? Where had the time gone?

It has been twenty years since my wife beat cancer, and I'm thankful every day. I still am working in real estate because I love helping people create the life they want. But my plan now includes goals and dreams and no longer centers around making a certain number of dollars. I live my life with much more purpose and carve out the time to be with my family and make memories. I took a saying by the Dalai Lama and changed it to best fit what I have learned about life and finances over my sixty-plus years of life: "Man sacrifices his health in order to make money. Then he sacrifices money to recuperate his health. And then he is so anxious about the future that he does not enjoy the present. The result being that he does not live in the present or the future. He lives as if he is never going to die and then dies having never really lived." I have watched far too many of my friends, relatives, and people in general fail to plan for their later years. I don't believe that happiness comes from having a huge pile of money because I don't believe you can buy happiness—it's an inside job. I do know, though, that nothing is free in life. So you do need a certain amount of money to pay for the freedom to spend your time doing whatever it is that truly makes you happy. We all start out trading our time for dollars so that we can pay for the necessities in life and the stuff we tend to accumulate. I do not believe we should buy into the idea of working until we are sixty-five or seventy years old, so we can retire and enjoy the good life. To break free of the bonds of a life dedicated to working until then, you need to do a couple of things. First, you have to accept the fact that you will need to take financial control of your future. Second, you must have a serious talk with yourself and figure out what it is that makes you happy. An easy way to do this is to pretend you won the lottery and start listing all the things you would do if you didn't have to work. This will change over time, but it will give you a start. Then you need to put a plan together on how you are going to get enough passive income from your investments so that you don't have to work every day.

FINANCIAL PLAN

MARTIN J. STONE

1. My goal is to accumulate $500,000. equity in real estate and business investments and $25,000. cash.

2. To achieve this goal I will have to devote as much time and effort as needed to keep my investments moving according to the plan I have proposed.

3. I plan to achieve this goal by age 35.

4. I plan to achieve this goal through real estate and business investments as outlined in the enclosed documents.

5. I've drafted a workable plan for my financial future to age 35. At that time I plan to have $500,000. equity in real estate and business holdings and $25,000. cash in the bank. I have made all the initial investments to carry out the plan except one which will be made before June, 1977. My efforts will be divided in two areas. First, I must maintain my real estate and keep the equities growing at the planned rates. Second, the major task will be promoting the growth of my business investment. This will require the maximum use of my time and the continual effort to improve my management ability and financial expertise.

1 Jan 74

M. J. Stone

Projected Financial Goals

| Nature of Asset Equity Only | Jan 74 | 1 Jan 75 | 1 Jan 76 | 1 Jan 77 | 1 Jan 78 | 1 Jan 79 |
|---|---|---|---|---|---|---|
| **Current Assets:** | | | | | | |
| Cash | 6,700 | 10,000 | 20,000 | 30,000 | 30,000 | 35,000 |
| Stocks/Bonds | 100 | 100 | 5,000 | 5,000 | 8,000 | 10,000 |
| **Long Term Assets:** | | | | | | |
| Notes | | 2,000 | 5,000 | 5,000 | 8,000 | 10,000 |
| Real Estate Owned | | 6,000 | 15,000 | 25,000 | 40,000 | 65,000 |
| Other Business Interest | | 3,000 / 28,200 | 5,000 / 40,600 | 8,000 / 53,000 | 10,000 / 62,000 | 15,000 / 80,000 |
| TOTAL ASSET EQUITY | 6,800 | 49,300 | 90,000 | 126,000 | 158,000 | 215,000 |

## PART 1

# Setting Your Dreams in Motion

# 1

# Building a Great Life

*"The highest use of capital is not to make money but to make money do more for the betterment of life."*
—Henry Ford

In the book *Invest in Yourself: Six Secrets to a Rich Life,* coauthor Marc Eisenson notes that once we become adults, "we often lose track of life's simple pleasures and of our own personal goals. We take a wrong turn or two, then spend a good portion of our lives doing things we'd rather not—while not doing the things we'd enjoy." He goes on: "While we may obsess about how unhappy we are, we don't focus clearly on what we can do to change the situation, on how we can invest our time, energy, and, yes, our money to consciously create the life we want."

In this chapter I want to accomplish three things. First, I want to help you get a handle on where you stand financially at this very moment. Second, I'll see what it will take to at least maintain your current lifestyle—how to generate that 80 to 100 percent of your current income needed once you're through working. Third, you'll do some realistic dreaming about the kind of life you'd truly like to have. Like Eisenson said, there are ways we can invest our time, energy, and money to consciously create the life we want. Here, in chapter one, you'll consciously start down that road.

## FOCUS UP

While this is a book about using real estate to create freedom in your life, the first goal is to get the attention of those who don't already "get" it and help them focus on making life enjoyable. Any investment we choose is just a tool to help generate the money necessary to find or pay for happiness. Investing in real estate is no different, for it will be a means to an end. It's like trading our time for dollars at our jobs. We don't get up every morning at six thirty to be at work by eight o'clock because we simply love entering data into a computer. Rather, we go to earn the money we need to generate the type of lifestyle we desire. It's an added bonus if we enjoy our jobs, but in the end it's all about the money.

As we get older, we learn that though our jobs may be about the money, our lives are certainly not. It's those priceless things that usually hold the most meaning: coaching our son in his first Little League game or watching our daughter in a ballet recital, wearing the dress we had the time to make. No, it's not just about the money. But, alas, money is the tool we need to obtain the things we really want. We may not like these rules, but they are the rules nonetheless.

At this point you're probably saying to yourself, "If it's not about the money, then why am I reading this book?" What I'm talking about is finding a balance in life. I want to strike a chord in you, so you will start actively thinking about creating something special for yourself in the future, as opposed to just living for the present.

## FINDING BALANCE

When most of us make comments about the rich, we usually say things like "Ah, they never have to work" or "They can do anything they want." Thus, we resent the wealthy without realizing that with a bit of planning our lives could be abundant as well. Success is about finding a balance between wanting what you don't have and being happy and content with what you do have. Poor people aren't always unhappy, and rich people aren't always happy.

Author Whit Hobbs says that "success is waking up in the morning, whoever you are, however old or young, and bouncing out of bed because there's something out there that you love to do. Something that you believe in, that you're good at—something that's bigger than you are, and you can hardly wait to get at it again." Hobbs doesn't talk about money or a job. He's talking about doing something every day that you love to do. Thus, money can't bring happiness. But it will provide the opportunity and wherewithal to find what you love to do.

It's the task of finding out where we would like to be that evades most of us. We get so caught up in surviving each day that we fail to make the time to remember what it is that really makes us happy. Worse yet, the things that probably would make us happy are with us daily, but we are so busy working at life that we fail to enjoy the happiness we do have. Remember the scene in *The Wizard of Oz* where everyone got their wish but Dorothy? The Tin Man was shown what a big heart he had; the Scarecrow realized that he was, indeed, the brains of the operation all along; and even the Cowardly Lion came to own his courage. For Dorothy, though, all hope seemed lost. That is until Glinda the Good Witch arrived. Glinda reminded Dorothy that she had been wearing the slippers that would take her home all along. Well, that's what we're talking about.

Isn't it possible that we're each wearing our own pair of ruby red slippers right now? To avoid chasing the wrong dreams, it's important to spend some time now determining what it is that will give you joy and contentment in the future. Like Dorothy, a bit of focused thought on what it is we want might just send us home again. This is a book about making the money to pay the toll of life. This toll will help us secure the freedom to enjoy what makes us happy.

## THREE KEY STEPS

Here are some strategies that should help in reaching your goals. Of course, these systems don't carry any guarantee, but by educating yourself you maximize your probability of success. The Boy Scouts got it right when they made their motto "Be prepared." This is advice that we all should take seriously for anything we do but especially when dealing with our future.

Besides being prepared, the following three steps must be adhered to when it comes to investing. Each step is essential, and each one builds on the other:

1. Grow your investments.

2. Protect your investments.

3. Enjoy the fruits of your investments.

Growing your investments is the first goal. The rub is that by growing our investments we must put off that all-too-common human trait to consume. As Americans, statistics show that the majority of us spend roughly 110 percent of what we bring in each month. No wonder we can't get ahead. Now is the time to rethink that behavior. The idea is to deny ourselves a few present-day pleasures to achieve some loftier and more important goals for the future.

Protecting your investments is the second task. Because any profit is the return we earn for taking some level of risk, one can never have a foolproof investment. Nonetheless, if we do our homework properly and stay vigilant, we will realize the highest probability of success in reaching our goals. Thankfully, this probability of success is especially true when it comes to investing in real estate.

Finally, enjoying the fruits of your investments is what it's all about. In life, nothing is worth it unless there is a payoff at the finish line. With investments, we call that payoff a profit. This is a critical component to the equation, but one that is all too often bypassed by the workaholic. For him or her and for many of the rest of us, we need to remember why we are trying to make those profits. It's easy to get caught up in the growing phase of our investments and never take time out to enjoy the fruits of our labor. This attitude is just as risky as the attitude of those who live only for today.

## DETERMINING NET WORTH

Before you can figure out where you're going, you should get a handle on where you sit financially today. The next few forms are pretty simple to fill out. The best way to find out where you are at this moment is to work up a balance sheet, which lists your assets and liabilities. Once you've completed your list, if you subtract your liabilities from your assets, the remainder will be your net worth. Your net worth is the sum total of what you have been able to save from all the money you have earned to date. Theoretically, these are the assets you will be able to put to work to earn money when you retire. This money plus Social Security and any existing company retirement plan you may have will be the beginning of your nest egg. Don't fret if you discover that your nest egg is nil or next to nil at this point. The idea is to assess where you are at this moment.

Because the goal of this book is to get you to take advantage of the benefits of real estate, we suggest you complete a standard Federal National Mortgage Association (aka FNMA or Fannie Mae) 1003 loan application. You can get one at almost any bank, mortgage broker, or savings and loan that makes home loans. These forms are the standard in the industry, and once put together with all the required schedules, they will save you a lot of time once you begin applying for real estate loans. Once completed, it will be easy to update any items that change over the years.

In lieu of a standard Fannie Mae loan application, you can start with the form in Figure 1.1 to help you determine your net worth.

Figure 1.1

## NET WORTH SUMMARY

Home Equity                                 $_____
   (value less loans)

Vehicle Equity                              $_____
   (value less loans; don't forget boats and toys)

Cash or Equivalents                         $_____
   (savings, checking, money markets, etc.)

Stocks, Bonds, Mutual Funds                 $_____

IRAs, Keoghs, 401(k)s                       $_____

Equity in Life Insurance                    $_____

Equity in Other Real Estate                 $_____
   (value less loans)

Equity in Your Business                     $_____

Art, Collections, Etc.                      $_____

Other Assets                                $_____

Total Net Worth                             $_____

## ASSETS VERSUS LIABILITIES

At this point it's important to think about assets and liabilities. The word *asset* implies something of value, as opposed to a liability, which refers to a debt. Regrettably, assets for retirement purposes are of value to you only if they provide a positive cash flow benefit. For instance, if you have a painting worth $5,000 hanging on a wall, it may give you pleasure, but that aside, it's of no value to your retirement fund. That is, of course, unless you're charging admission to your neighbors for viewings. This is a primary concept you must understand: unless the money you invest makes money, it becomes a liability.

The biggest negative value most of us have is our home. Sadly, like the Monet on your wall, the net equity from your home is of no value for retirement because it doesn't produce any spendable return. Furthermore, making the payment for taxes, insurance, upkeep, and a possible mortgage becomes a drain on the other incomes you have. Again, this negative drain makes your home a liability.

The concept of considering a home a liability rather than an asset on a balance sheet is the most controversial and hotly debated subject I encounter in my business. But, remember, our goal is to help you create enough income from real estate, so you can afford all the dreams you care to pursue. To that end, this may require you to use the asset value of your home to jump-start your investment program.

If this thought gives you initial pause, just recall the statistics we quoted in the introduction. Ninety-five percent of all Americans retire practically broke! If anything should scare you, this should. And because a good percentage of Americans own their home, this statistic tells us that our home ownership could be in serious jeopardy if we don't do something to protect it before it's too late. My goal isn't to talk you out of your home. Rather, I want you to earn enough, so you can always live wherever you want.

## BACK TO THE FUTURE

Next, I want to help you determine where you will be when it comes time for you to retire or, better yet, claim your freedom. I will make this review very simple. Again, my goal is to get you thinking about this subject, enough to give you an elementary education on what lies ahead.

The two main problems with predicting where you will be when you retire are:

1. inflation; and

2. job stability.

Over time, inflation rates can change like the wind. In fact, at certain times inflation can actually be a friend, not a foe. You will learn later that if you have a lot of levered real estate in an inflationary time, your estate will grow at an astronomical rate. But if you've converted all your assets to cash and are trying to live off that in a low inflationary time, you're probably experiencing some financial problems. For this reason we're going to try to determine where you will be in the future, measured in today's dollars, by factoring in 3 percent to account for inflation.

Estimating what you can expect from your pension plan can be a tough proposition. Because many companies seem to be disappearing at an alarming rate, it makes us wonder if those plans have any more value than depending on Social Security. One of my main goals is to help you recognize the shortcomings of relying on Social Security and your company pension plan. To help with that goal, I recommend you seek out what someone in your position would receive monetarily right now if he or she retired today with the number of years you will have on that job when you retire. You may need to make a few adjustments, but the idea is to get a ballpark figure on the monthly amount.

Our goal from this exercise is specific. It's to make an estimate of any shortfall in retirement income if you don't do anything different from what you are already doing. I will then convert that shortfall to a lump-sum dollar figure (see Figure 1.2). This will give you a concrete goal to shoot for in your planning. To make this easy, I suggest you make it your goal to replace 100 percent of your current income.

To estimate that lump sum, I am going to assume you will net only 3 percent on it. At the writing of this book, CD (certificate of deposit) rates have been below 2 percent. With taxes and inflation, this certainly hasn't been a good time for cash investments. Surely this will improve, but if you're trying to sustain a twenty- to thirty-year retirement fund, I feel being conservative is best.

You can obtain more accurate information on your Social Security benefits by contacting them directly at (800) 772-1213 or at its website www.ssa.gov.

FIGURE 1.2

**RETIREMENT INCOME WORKSHEET**

1. Annual Income Goal                                    $_____
   (100% of your current income)

2. Estimated Social Security Benefits    $_____

3. Estimated Pension Benefits                $_____

4. Retirement Income Gap                      $_____
   (subtract lines 2 and 3 from line 1)

5. Lump Sum Needed                              $_____
   (divide amount on line 4 by .03)

6. Current Retirement Assets               $_____
   (IRA, 401(k), and other sources)

7. Total Lump-Sum Gap                         $_____
   (subtract line 6 from line 5)

This exercise is oversimplified to provide a basic understanding of what kind of retirement nest egg you are going to need. By relating the monthly income needed to a lump sum, I hope to help you visualize the task that lies ahead.

Many of you will have various types of assets that will provide you with a retirement income. Assets are great, but when you are retired and not bringing in a paycheck, all that really counts is the monthly income those assets may generate. If you have a lot of equity in your home and a valuable art collection you would rather not sell, neither can be used in calculating your lump-sum gap. In reality, these kinds of assets usually just increase the gap.

The following exercise is one that I hope will get you to act and invest differently. In all likelihood, if you've been working for twenty years and have accumulated a large deficit on the lump-sum line of the Retirement Income Worksheet in Figure 1.2, you're probably not going to accumulate the balance you need to retire. If you continue to do what you have done, you will be one of the 95 percent who are broke at retirement. Yes, you can sell the home or the paintings, but we don't believe you need to do that if you begin to invest properly for your retirement.

Not only do I not want you to sell your home, I want you to start thinking about all the additional things you would like to have or do if you were retired and had the time and money. I'm not just talking about dreaming here, I'm talking about dreaming big! For many of you, that lump-sum gap may seem so large that you're thinking it would be completely foolish to fantasize about other things. Nothing could be further from the truth. Aspirations are what make us truly live. We don't work hard because work is fun; we work hard to get the money to pay for the things that make us happy. The Reverend Robert Schuller said, "It's unfulfilled dreams that keep us alive."

Don't be discouraged if that lump-sum gap seems so huge that you'd feel foolish even thinking about "the better things in life." I have found that it's easier for most of us to sacrifice for something we "want to have" as opposed to something we "should be doing." We should all save money every month, but do we? If you fall in love with that new car, just think how easy it is to justify that extra $200 a month to pay for it. In twenty years that car will be paid off and worth just a few thousand dollars. Rather than buy the car, if you had committed to putting the $200 in a bank account each month for those twenty years, you would have accumulated $48,000 by now.

Sit down with a paper and pen or at your computer and start listing all the things you would like to enjoy when you retire. Don't forget anything. Henry David Thoreau said, "In the long run, men hit only what they aim at. Therefore, though they should fail immediately, they had better aim at something high." Aim high, so if you miss a few things along the way, you'll still be a big winner. Figure 1.3 is a sample wish list and an estimate of what these kinds of dreams may cost.

FIGURE 1.3

**SAMPLE WISH LIST**

| Dreams | Cost |
|---|---|
| Cabin | $100,000 |
| Pleasure Boat | $25,000 |
| New Car | $45,000 |
| Country Club Membership | $25,000 |

| Weekly Golf: $125/round for 10 Years | $65,000 |
|---|---|
| Vacations: 4/year @ $2,500 Each for 10 Years | $100,000 |
| College for Grandchildren: 3 @ $25,000 | $75,000 |
| Total Cost of Dreams | $435,000 |

Think I'm crazy? You already have a lump-sum gap, and now I'm talking about adding $435,000 to that figure! Here's an example of how compound interest and appreciation can increase your returns. Let's say you have just twenty years to go before you retire and you determine you're short $100,000 on the lump sum. What's more, you now need to find another $435,000 to fund your wish list. Well, if you could get your hands on $30,000 to invest in real estate today and keep it growing at 20 percent per year for the next twenty years, your nest egg would grow to $1,150,128. We'd then discount that money at 3 percent to cover for inflation, and you still would have accumulated $636,798 in today's currency. This amount of money definitely covers your lump-sum shortfall and still leaves you with a $100,000-plus cushion.

This initial investment amount will get you a decent property in most states in the country. Using an FHA owner-occupied loan, you could purchase a property up to about $850,000, and even in Southern California that could be a nice four-unit building.

Is this guaranteed? Of course not. But would you rather take a chance on funding a comfortable retirement now and fulfilling your dreams, or would you rather just wait to wind up in the 95 percent broke group once you retire? This book is dedicated to giving you the best shot at obtaining your goals, using real estate as the vehicle to get there.

"Over twenty years ago my husband and I sat down with Marty and listened to the possibilities that rental property had to offer. He educated us on the ins and outs of investing and how things would work to our benefit over time. There were charts and graphs all over the walls showing the long-term benefits in owning investment property. It was not a huge jump to us as we had both grown up with parents having rental properties.

We started looking at a few properties.  Marty worked up the return on investment numbers for us, and how the investment would grow for us over time. I was blown away on the long term forecast and thought "oh if only . . ." Well I am here to tell you it has exceeded our expectations.

Over the years it started to all come to fruition. Eleven apartment buildings later we are able to retire early on the monthly passive income."

—*Leslie R.*

# —— CRITICAL CONCEPT ——

## Ownership of Property

It's not the property that makes you wealthy; it's the ownership of it that does. I hope you will see how wealth is created by the economic factors I'll be discussing and not because of the specific property you buy or the "great deal" you believe you struck. The reality is the best way to pick a property is to look for the one that best fits the goals you have in your plan. Once you have established your goals and have committed a certain amount of capital to them, it is usually not that difficult to find a clean, well-located property that will meet those aims. The best way to think about property is to understand that it is only a tool to help you accomplish your objectives. You are not buying an apartment building because you want to own an apartment building; you are buying it because it will help you accomplish your purposes.

# 2

# Setting Achievable Goals

*"October: This is one of the particularly dangerous months to invest in stocks. Other dangerous months are July, January, September, April, November, May, March, June, December, August, and February."*
　　　　　　　　　　　　　　　　　　　—Mark Twain

I've spent some time imploring you to take charge of your financial future. In the old days, people talked about working until they were sixty-five years old and then retiring. Nowadays, many clients speak about working until they are seventy. At our company, we take the opposite view. If you can figure out how much you need to live a happy, contented life and you can achieve that sooner than later, why not go for it?

## STRIKING IT RICH

You've probably noticed that I've yet to talk about getting rich. This is because getting rich is really a state of mind based on your definition of the word. *Rich* implies reaching a goal of obtaining a certain amount of money rather than actually achieving true desires and needs for you and your family. What's more, for an adult who is truly grounded, striking gold without hitting the lottery is simply beyond the realm of what is possible.

Now contrast "getting rich" with "practically broke." "Practically broke" is something many of us can remember, probably because we've all been there at one time or another. Truth be told, once we are no longer "practically broke," we never want to go back. We get a good job, start making decent money, and life is good. Even so, regardless of the variation on this theme, most of us believe that if we work hard enough, the American dream will materialize. We want to envision a retirement that could include second homes, golf vacations, water toys, and money to spare to help our grandchildren with their education. These types of perks may seem like pipe dreams, but they are absolutely attainable if you invest in real estate. Just ask anyone who's taken a chance and dipped their toes in this pool of water.

## THREE GROUPS OF INVESTORS

To help distinguish the actions needed to achieve your dreams, I'll begin by categorizing you into one of three different groups. These groups are differentiated by the amount of years you have left to work and, conversely, by the number of years you'll be able to let your investments grow before you retire. Of course, everyone's story is different, but by picking three broad stages, we hope that everyone might find enough similarities in one of the groups to find a place to begin. These groups are:

1. "Got Plenty of Time." These people are in their twenties or early thirties and are just getting started working. For them, the world is their oyster. They believe they can accomplish anything they set their minds to. Best of all, they have the benefit of time to help make their dreams come true.

2. "Too Busy Just Hangin' On." These are Gen Xers who are in the middle of their working lives. They have families, mortgages, and worries. Their prayer is that Social Security, a boom in the stock market, the company pension plan, or their children will help fill the bill when their retirement comes. Their big fear is that they won't.

3. "Worried It May Be Too Late." This is the over-fifty crowd, and when it comes to retirement, they're scared to death. Statistics show that once they retire they'll probably have to go back to work as a greeter at their local Walmart to make ends meet. Time is running out and they know it.

Thankfully, there is hope and, better yet, solutions for each of these groups. I have helped countless people in the

"Worried It May Be Too Late" group fund comfortable retirements through real estate investing. We'll begin by talking to those who've "got plenty of time."

## GROUP #1: "GOT PLENTY OF TIME"

We really don't get any smarter as we grow older. Rather, we just gain experience from messing up so many times and not listening when we were younger. But the lessons we've learned haven't been all too different from those we learned in school. For example, in math class we learned that $2 + 2 = 4$. In the school of life, we also learn about math— specifically. that too many credit-card payments can get you in a world of hurt. This is especially true when you're out of work or at any type of crossroads. A key difference between schoolhouse lessons and life lessons is that when you learn lessons in the real world, you tend to pay a bit closer attention. One reason is real-world lessons often hit you where it hurts most: in the wallet.

In the movie *The Natural*, Glenn Close said, "We all have the life we learn with and the life we live with after that." We say you can decide to take your full measure of life and learn everything the hard way, or you can pay attention to what those who came before you have to pass on. Thankfully, there is good news: if you fit into the "Got Plenty of Time" group, you can accomplish almost anything you put your mind to. This is primarily true because you have the time, which will escape you once you get older. Time to make mistakes, time to fix them, time to invest and, best of all, time to let your investments grow. If you use this time wisely, you surely will be able to live your dreams, not just dream about them.

Many people starting out feel like they have been misled by older people who didn't take advantage of the opportunities the United States of America has to offer. In truth, maybe some of the grown-ups in their lives were just a bit scared and therefore played it too safe along the way. Someone once said that you know you're old when your dreams turn to regrets. Napoleon Hill, the acclaimed author of *Think and Grow Rich*, couldn't disagree more. He said, "Cherish your visions and your dreams as they are the children of your soul, the blueprints of your ultimate achievements."

For those who've "got plenty of time," your financial future is like a rocket on a launchpad. However, it's up to you to decide what type of rocket you want. Think about the rocket that launches the space shuttle. It leaves the launchpad slowly, builds up speed, and then boosts the shuttle into orbit. As the photographs taken from the shuttle show, the view from up there is breathtaking. In contrast, a bottle rocket takes off very fast, rises a short distance, and then fizzles out and drops to earth. Ninety-five percent of those who retire in our country are like bottle rockets; only 5 percent are taking in that great view. True, they're not orbiting the earth from the space shuttle, but the view from the clubhouse at Pebble Beach in California is just as breathtaking.

As you begin making money, it's tempting to spend not only the money you earn today but also to borrow on what you will make in the future: lots of dinners out on your charge card, a new car every few years, a big-screen TV financed at the credit union, and a tax refund loan to pay for a summer getaway. Yes, you can afford it. The problem is you get used to spending most (or all) of what you earn and not putting any away for your future. If this is you, you're headed for trouble.

To succeed and take advantage of real estate investing to help you reach your dreams, I'm going to assume you are financially qualified to invest and you'll agree to make a few small sacrifices early on. From there, I'll show you where those small sacrifices might take you from an investment standpoint. And because we don't want you to think you will have to sacrifice forever, I am going to be working with just some of your earnings for the next five years. I'll make the following assumptions: you can save enough each year from your earnings and tax refund to invest $5,000 a year for those first five years. Additionally, instead of buying that new $25,000 car on credit, you will put the same amount as the payment into a savings account each month, to be invested in year six.

The following numbers come from using the compound interest formula to project your future net worth based on various rates of return. The table shows how your investments can grow at two modest rates of return. We used a 20 percent and a 25 percent compound rate of return on equity for these examples. The grand total numbers might seem astronomical, especially if you're used to looking at typical rates of return from CDs or stocks or mutual funds. But remember, real estate benefits from leverage and leverage is what puts real estate investing into a stratosphere by itself. Because of this, fairly modest cash rates of return improve at an exceedingly rapid pace. Here's the idea:

| Year | Amount | Years Invested | 20% Return | 25% Return |
|---|---|---|---|---|
| 1 | $5,000 | 25 | $ 476,981 | $ 1,323,489 |
| 2 | $5,000 | 24 | $ 397,484 | $ 1,058,791 |
| 3 | $5,000 | 23 | $ 331,237 | $ 847,033 |
| 4 | $5,000 | 22 | $ 276,031 | $ 677,626 |
| 5 | $5,000 | 21 | $ 230,026 | $ 542,101 |
| 6 | $25,000 | 20 | $ 958,440 | $2,168,405 |
| **Grand Total** | | | $2,670,199 | $ 6,617,445 |

Go ahead and pinch yourself. It's okay. Who would ever have thought that by investing in property today, you could generate between $2,000,000 to $6,500,000 in twenty-five years? What's more, you achieved this by just making one $5,000 investment a year for five years and delayed buying a brand-new car for a while. Yes, of course these numbers are staggering and, yes, of course it will take work. However, achieving a return like this through investing in real estate is really just a combination of three elements. Big-time real estate investors are aware of these elements, and now so are you. They are:

1. leverage;

2. compound interest; and

3. time.

Is this return on your investment guaranteed? Of course not. But is this type of return from an investment in real estate a very good possibility? Most certainly. In fact, if you get serious about this game, it's not only possible, it's probable. What you have to ask yourself is if you want to take your chances on Social Security and your employer's pension plan being enough. Or do you want to ensure that you'll be in the 5 percent who are financially independent at retirement by making a few small and smart real estate investments now? The decision should be an easy one.

## GROUP #2: "TOO BUSY JUST HANGIN' ON"

For Gen Xers in the middle of their working lives who are "too busy just hangin' on," life may seem like you're on a runaway train. You're headed down a mountain, don't have any brakes, and God only knows if you'll survive. If you're old enough to remember the Ed Sullivan variety show on television, the host often featured a guest who would spin multiple plates on sticks. This guy had plates spinning above his hands, plates spinning from his feet and, to top it off, plates spinning from a stick in his mouth. Of course, you see where this story is going. Inevitably, he couldn't keep all the plates spinning and one by one they would each fall and crash to the ground. Sound a little like your life? It's not that you don't make good money. Rather, no matter how much you make, there just never seems to be enough to go around. You've got responsibilities: the house, food, kids, clothes, cars, entertainment, soccer camp, music lessons, cleaning, cell phones, cable TV, and on and on.

At this stage in your life, you've begun to think about retirement. More accurately, you're beginning to get tired of the daily grind and are secretly wishing for an early retirement. The trouble is you're concerned, rightfully, about where the money to retire might come from. Maybe your 401(k) or company pension account has taken a hit and you're finally deciding it's time to pay more attention to the future. Great, I've been pitching self-reliance, so this is a fine spot to be in. For you, the good news is you can still make a big difference in your retirement picture.

If you followed the numbers in the chart for the "Got Plenty of Time" folks, those same numbers will work for you too. The difference is that, unlike them, you're not too excited about working for another twenty-five-plus years. If you're in your mid-forties, you've probably been working for fifteen to twenty years so far and are looking at retiring in no more than another fifteen to twenty years. However, the reality is if you don't make some changes right now, you'll be working until you're sixty-five or seventy—not because you want to, but because you need to just to make ends meet. It doesn't have to be that way.

If you understand the story I'm telling, you are now well aware of the challenges that lay ahead. Best yet, you want to do something about it. This is good. Unfortunately, because you're on that runaway train doing what you always did, a way out seems like a fading dream. Well, it's not just a dream.

Here are a few ideas, which if you put into practice, can make big differences in your life and retirement.

The first principle makes a distinction between *wants* and *needs*. These words seem so simple, but they can be used in enough different ways that they can be confusing. In this society, we seem to be motivated by our wants rather than by the desire to just satisfy our needs. What do we mean? The thought *I want a new BMW* motivates many people to work a little overtime or justify going $50,000 into debt, so they can buy one. The fact is their perfectly good Chevy that's paid for does a fine job getting them to and from work every day. Sure, a new BMW would be nice, but it won't do anything to help secure a comfortable future for you and your family.

The dilemma gets more complicated as we age and take on new responsibilities. Do we spend $5,000 on a new pool table for the game room or make sure that money is set aside into our kids' college funds? Clearly, the ability to pick the need instead of the want is the biggest initial step in breaking through to a new future. I'm sure you realize that most of these decisions in life involve money. If you buy the new BMW instead of driving the paid-for Chevy, your wallet will be that much lighter every month. The truth is either way, in five years, all you'll have is a used car.

If this was just a one-shot decision, I wouldn't be mentioning this concept. But it's not. It's your way of thinking about money and spending and saving that has to change. It's about where you shop for almost everything you buy.

Do you mow your own lawn for the exercise or do you pay someone to do it and pay an additional $35 per month to a gym that you don't use? Do you iron your own shirts while watching TV or send them out? Three years of sending your shirts out to be cleaned at $1.25 each costs $937.50. This $937.50 would be the FHA down payment on a $30,000 property. In many parts of the country, $30,000 will buy a decent home. Are you getting the point?

Now try substituting the word *greed* for *want*, and the decision becomes one of greed versus need. If you think about all the things you've bought when you spent more than you needed to, you'll probably come to the same conclusion that I have about most items: that is the wanting brought you more enjoyment than the having.

In fact, for an exercise, conduct a complete financial review of yourself. Write down all the areas each month where you spend money. Many of your expenses will be completely legitimate. Others, however, will strike you as frivolous and a complete waste. The goal is to find areas where you could save by fulfilling needs instead of wants. You don't have to give up all the nice things in life. You only need to sacrifice a little bit now, so you can have a lot later.

Ralph Waldo Emerson said, "There is really no insurmountable barrier save your own inherent weakness of purpose." To that end, sell the BMW and pay cash for a used Chevy. Sell the motor home and buy a tent. Iron those shirts, mow the lawn, and cut your cable. Refinance the house and pull out some money to invest. What I want you to do is substitute needs for wants, so you can find the money to invest in your future. It's critical that you give yourself a shot at being in the 5 percent group who will have a comfortable future to look forward to.

In the following table I'm going to give you examples of what some small sacrifices might do for you. Again, I'm using the compound interest formula to arrive at these numbers. We'll use different initial amounts of money and determine where they will take you in the remaining twenty years or so you have left to work. Those of you in this "Too Busy Just Hangin' On" group have a distinct advantage over the "Got Plenty of Time" younger group. You've worked for ten or fifteen years and have that experience and knowledge when you surmise, "If I were only twenty-five again and know what I know today." I can't make you twenty-five once more, but instead I want you to take a deep breath, think long and hard about what you've learned about "doing it the way you always have," and take advantage of capitalism. If you do, you can make yourself and your family some real money—the kind that could put you on the path to comfort in your future.

| Amount | Years Invested | 20% Return | 25% Return |
|--------|----------------|------------|------------|
| $5,000 | 20 | $ 191,700 | $ 433,700 |
| $10,000 | 20 | $ 383,400 | $ 867,400 |
| $25,000 | 20 | $ 958,440 | $ 2,168,405 |
| $50,000 | 20 | $ 1,916,880 | $ 4,336,810 |

As I said before, with real estate investing, these numbers are not only possible but probable.

## GROUP #3: "WORRIED IT MAY BE TOO LATE"

Personally, I have yet to enter into the "Worried It May Be Too Late" group. I do, however, completely understand your concerns because I have helped countless families, friends, and clients like you deal with the financial challenges that go with planning for people who are closer to actual retirement. Though it may seem like it, it is definitely not too late to make a real difference in your picture. A key advantage for you is you have a world of experience to draw from.

In 1954, Ray Kroc, a traveling Multimixer salesman, signed a contract to use the hamburger-selling ideas of the McDonald brothers to open a few places of his own. In his book, *Grinding It Out,* Kroc describes himself as "a battle-scarred veteran of the business wars." He hadn't graduated from high school, had been working for more than thirty years, and was battling diabetes and arthritis and the effects of losing his gall bladder and most of his thyroid. At the time he began his burger empire, he was fifty-two years old. For most of us, fifty-two is when we want to start slowing down. Starting a business that we knew nothing about wouldn't even enter our minds. Nonetheless, for Kroc the rest is history. By 1976, McDonald's would surpass $1 billion in total revenue. It took IBM and Xerox forty-six years and sixty-three years, respectively, to reach that mark.

I'm not suggesting you become a hamburger mogul, but I do want you to realize what is possible for those on the latter end of their working lives. Kroc's story is incredible; you probably won't duplicate it. What I want is for you to seize the opportunity this country has to offer, so you can live the happy ending to your story. In the words of a French proverb, "To believe a thing impossible is to make it so."

I began this section with some words about risk and excessive caution. In all likelihood, if you're not comfortable now, it's probably because you didn't take a couple of chances at success when you were younger. Alternatively, perhaps you did take some chances, but for one reason or another they just didn't work out. My ideas and this book are meant to give you some concrete ways to give it another try. Helen Keller said, "When one door of opportunity closes, another opens. But often we look so long at the closed door that we do not see the one which has opened for us."

At this stage of your life, having clear-cut financial goals is of paramount importance. For you, it will be somewhat easier to complete the charts we provided earlier because you're already staring retirement in the eye. Remember that statistically your life span is getting longer every year. If you're sixty-five years old, your life expectancy is 84.3 for men and 86.7 for women. That's a long time to be alive with no job to go to and no money to help you enjoy your free time.

For anyone in this category, your most important goal will be to focus on creating spendable income that is hedged against inflation. You definitely should have some reserves in the bank for emergencies, but because of the effects of inflation, savings-type investments tend to have diminishing value. In fact, the rates of return these types of investments pay after taxes are usually just about at the rate of inflation. So if you spend the interest income, the purchasing power of the savings nest egg decreases each year. I believe that the best place to find inflation-hedging cash flow is from owning rental property. Most of the remainder of this book will be dedicated to helping you understand how to take full advantage of this kind of investment.

If you're in the "Worried It May Be Too Late" group, the real secret to being successful will come from a change in your focus. The strategies I laid out for the first two groups, "Got Plenty of Time" and "Too Busy Just Hangin' On," were centered on overcoming shortfalls in the nest egg and building toward dreams for an eventual retirement. Instead of long-term wealth-building, this third group has to focus directly on creating cash flow *now* to live day to day. At this point it's not about the percentage return that's important; it's an actual monthly cash return that needs to be your real focal point.

The best way to achieve this goal is to either pay all cash for a building or, alternatively, put down at least a sizable amount of money to minimize any mortgage payment. However, if you can work at least ten more years, you still have time to take advantage of some amount of leverage. Your goal will be to find one or more properties that will provide you with the greatest cash flow at that retirement point. Because the most conservative goal is to have that property paid off by the time you retire, let's work toward that end.

An ideal property would be one with an assumable loan that would be fully amortized (paid off) the month you retire. It even would be better if the down payment was exactly the same as your investment nest egg. I know this doesn't always happen, so here are a few ideas that can help you get close.

1. I have found that most mortgages that are at least ten years old pay off principal at a fairly rapid clip. Also, by making an additional principal payment each month, most of these loans can be paid off in about half the time as the current payoff date. In many cases, any cash flow from the property could be enough to help accomplish that task. The more you focus on sound management, the faster you can get that loan paid off.

2. If you can't find a property you can pay off on its own merits, you may have to help it along when you retire. It may not work out for you to live in your rental building, so one solution might be to sell the big house and buy a smaller property in a retirement area. You can use some of the extra proceeds from the sale to pay off the balance of the mortgage, or you can reduce it enough so you can get it paid off very soon after retirement.

3. If you are in a limited down payment situation, you may have to count on leverage. Leverage can produce some huge equity gains over a number of years, but more risk is involved than with the conservative steps I've been discussing. This means you will have to use a higher leverage purchase like those offered by FHA, allowing you to buy with only .035% down on up to four units that you will occupy as an owner. So you follow a five- to ten-year growth-oriented program to build the biggest nest egg you can. The goal will be to sell at retirement and move that money into high cash flow, nonleveraged property. You will have to pay some taxes to accomplish the goal, but planning with your certified public accountant or tax expert can minimize that.

Finally, I want to debunk the myth of the "free and clear" house. Burning that mortgage is probably one of the major goals most of us have after paying on that property for twenty to thirty years. While it might be great to have the place paid off, that house is really the largest wasted asset most of us will possess in our lifetime. This is because the large equity you have in it, though it does provide you with a warm fuzzy feeling all over, doesn't produce any spendable income for you. We're well aware that to suggest that you sell the family home is about as popular as burning the flag. You may not need to sell it to improve your lifestyle, but you do need to start thinking about it as an asset, not just as your home. Here are a few ideas that should help.

For starters, if you were game and didn't need as much room anymore, selling your home would be by far the smartest business move you could make. With tax laws as they exist today, there would be no capital gain on the profit for selling your home up to $250,000 if you're single or up to $500,000 if you're married. This could be a tremendous way to create a retirement nest egg out of nothing. The good news is you can use this tax rule to your advantage over and over again as long as you follow the rules.

If, however, you are committed to keeping your house (and it is perfectly okay if you are), you should look into refinancing it to generate the cash necessary to invest in income property. At this point, if you've had your loan for many years, a large portion of your payment is probably going toward paying off the loan. This is called "principal reduction." In most cases, you can take out a new loan and keep your payment close to the same as it currently is.

Another added attraction is your tax benefits from your home will increase because the interest part of your payment will now be higher. Remember: you can't deduct the portion of your payment that goes toward principal, only the interest portion.

The table that follows may give you some examples of the kind of cash flow you might expect from the funds you take out of your home. The percentages are the cash-on-cash return from the amount invested in the property. The amount invested is the down payment, which is the number on the left-hand side of the chart. The dollar figure under the percentages is the estimated annual cash flow.

| Amount Invested | Estimated Annual Cash Flow | | |
|---|---|---|---|
| | 10% | 15% | 20% |
| $ 25,000 | $ 2,500 | $ 3,750 | $ 5,000 |
| $ 50,000 | $ 5,000 | $ 7,500 | $ 10,000 |
| $ 100,000 | $ 10,000 | $ 15,000 | $ 20,000 |
| $ 150,000 | $ 15,000 | $ 22,500 | $ 30,000 |

For most of us who ended up with a larger home for the family, this extra space really isn't needed once the kids leave home. The most practical move for parents without kids in the house anymore is to find a smaller, more economical place to live. In most areas, small- to medium-size investment properties include very nice owners' units. With a reasonable down payment, these properties can provide a nice place to live for a minimum monthly cost. Better yet, based on your down payment, they may even provide a free place to live plus some positive cash flow.

For those of you who don't own yet, it's time to get busy and buy some small units. Many programs are available that will allow you to buy a piece of property with little or no down payment, including FHA and VA (Department of Veterans Affairs) loans. I recommend you buy a small set of rental properties, something with two, three, or four units. This way you will have the best chance of a controllable cost of living that can decrease as you raise rents over the years. There are also some tax benefits and equity growth from appreciation and loan payoff.

The other issue to contend with is natural conservatism, which we all seem to gravitate toward as we get older. It's an offshoot of losing that invincibility of youth. We've learned the hard way that things don't always work out as we wanted or planned. What's more, some of those hard lessons cost us dearly. From a financial point of view, we frequently hear the following: "I don't want to take any chances with what I have because I'm too old." Or "I don't have the ability to make the money back." In principle I agree. But as a wise woman once said, "Take risks. You can't fall off the bottom."

**I'm not suggesting you risk all your savings on a long shot at the racetrack or you buy lottery tickets. I'm suggesting you dedicate some of your energies and money to beginning a new chapter in your life. If you do your homework, it will be very rewarding financially. Equally important, it may give you a new interest in life and something to do when you've got the gold watch and the boot from your day job.**

———— $ ————

"Because of difficulties I had encountered with owning real estate in other areas, I was reluctant to invest again. Buckingham's approach of focusing on education, getting to know the market, and sound investment strategies, made me feel comfortable enough to invest again. After the first purchase, it was much easier moving into other investment opportunities."

—*Paul*

# —— CRITICAL CONCEPT ——

## Compound Interest and Wealth Creation

Most things in life with a good payoff include risk.

Do you remember when you opened your first bank account and the banker explained to you that if you leave the interest you earn in the bank instead of spending it, your bank account balance will grow? If you apply this concept to grown-up money and you put in $100,000 at 3 percent for ten years, you would end up with $138,419. Your profit is $38,419.

The balance of the book is dedicated to showing you all the areas of return that you receive from owning investment property. Those returns are cash flow, equity growth from repayment of your loan, tax benefits, and appreciation in value. These can vary depending on the property you buy, the current economy, and the area of the country you are in, but over the long haul most investors can maintain an annual return of 20 percent to 25 percent. If this return seems high to you, the way I get this number will be fully explained in later chapters.

So you can see what compound interest can do for your money, this is what the $100,000 could grow to in ten years with the higher annual return from real estate investing:

$100,000 at 20% for 10 years = $619,173
$100,000 at 25% for 10 years = $931,322

If you want to play around with the $100,000, go to www.easysurf.cc/vfpt2.htm#fva, which has a calculator.

# 3

# Appreciation: The Big Lie

*"What one man can do, another can do."*

—Sir Anthony Hopkins in *The Edge*

I began this book at the end of the story—that is where you might be when it comes time to retire. I did so to emphasize what might happen if you wait much longer to examine this issue.

Again, there are no guarantees. As with any type of investment, you earn a return because there is some element of risk. You can put $10,000 under your mattress, but you won't earn any profit because you are supposedly taking risk out of the equation. But are you really? Your house could burn down or you could get robbed. You get the point: your money isn't safe even under a mattress.

Real estate, though, is historically one of the safest investments you can make because it is a tangible asset and one in which you can become the captain of your own ship.

Nonetheless, ungrounded fear of losing money keeps most people from ever getting started. I have, however, tried to turn the tables on you. I've told you what will likely happen if you don't invest, and it's not a pretty picture. Nonetheless, the outlook for those who are on board is bright. To that end, let's look at some property and play the Appreciation Game.

## REAL-LIFE EXAMPLE PROPERTY

Figure 3.1 shows the financial breakdown of a real property that I will use throughout the rest of the book as an example. It consists of four units in Long Beach, California. It is an entry-level city for first-time investors. Note that these are actual numbers from a real property taken from the Greater South Bay Regional Multiple Listing Service.

FIGURE 3.1

**EXAMPLE PROPERTY FROM 1992**

Property
Address:                          252 Cerritos Avenue
                                  Long Beach, California
Number of Units:                  4 units
Unit Mix:                         4 1-bedroom units
Year Built:                       1923

Property Financial Parameters
Purchase Price:                   $179,500
Monthly Income                    $2,200
(4 1-bedrooms, $550:
Equity:                           $35,900
Monthly Expenses:                 $660

Existing Encumbrances

| | |
|---|---|
| First Trust Deed Amount: | $143,600 |
| Interest Rate: | 8.0% |
| Years of Loan: | 30 |
| Monthly Payment: | $1,057 |

Miscellaneous Parameters

| | |
|---|---|
| Appreciation Rate: | 5.0% |
| Land Value: | $45,000 |
| Depreciable Improvements: | $134,500 |
| Expenses @ 30% | $7,920 |

## REAL-LIFE COMPARABLE PROPERTY SALE

Now that you see the financial parameters of the example property, what follows is the actual information from the sale of a comparable four-unit from the same neighborhood (just six blocks away) (Figure 3.2). We'll look at what happened to the value of these properties when we examine them in a twenty-five-year time span. The idea now is to illustrate what the Appreciation Game is really all about.

FIGURE 3.2

### COMPARABLE PROPERTY SALE FROM 2017

| Property | |
|---|---|
| Address: | 241 West 8th Street Long Beach, California |
| Number of Units: | 4 units |
| Unit Mix: | 4  1-bedroom units |
| Year Built: | 1918 |

Property Financial Parameters

| | |
|---|---|
| Purchase Price: | $729,500 |
| Monthly Income | $4,800 |
| (4 1-bedrooms, $1200): | |
| Equity: | $182,500 |
| Monthly Expenses: | $1,440 |

Existing Encumbrances

| | |
|---|---|
| First Trust Deed Amount: | $547,000 |
| Interest Rate: | 4.25% |
| Years of Loan: | 30 |
| Monthly Payment: | $2,691 |

Miscellaneous Parameters

| | |
|---|---|
| Appreciation Rate: | 5% |
| Land Value: | $180,000 |
| Depreciable Improvements: | $549,500 |
| Expenses @ 30% | $17,280 |

This is a real-life picture of what investing in this property would mean today for the person who bought it in 1992. For this investor, the property that cost $179,500 garnered an updated market value of $729,500 twenty-five years later. That is an increase in value of $550,000. Note that these numbers weren't made up; they are based on actual sales that took place between comparable properties in this average community.

I can make some calculations and project what the financial summary for this property would look like today.

I will assume our investor was conservative, so excess cash flow was used to pay off the loan in twenty-five years.

Market Value      $729,500
Loan Balances     $0
Equity Position   $729,500
Cash Flow         $3,360/month

The first impact of this free and clear property is the way it affects our conservative investor's balance sheet. This is a property with a market value of $729,500—that's three quarters of a million dollars! According to www.moneyrelationship.com, the average person has only $232,000 in net worth at retirement, so this one investment would put you over that figure.

The more important number for a conservative, retirement-oriented investor is how this type of investment creates a significant monthly income stream.

As I'm sure you would agree, this estimated monthly net income of $3,360 would certainly help create a nice retirement cushion.

Of course, our investor's $3,360 positive cash flow per month is no fortune by any stretch of the imagination; however, combined with other retirement income, the fruits of this $35,900 investment from 1992 are obvious. Additionally, this income is a hedge against inflation, for this property owner can pass any inflationary increase along to his or her tenants by gradually raising the rents over the years.

I want to show you where you might be in the future from a nest-egg position, assuming you bought a property like 241 West 8th Street in Long Beach, California, today. To calculate such a projection, we must know how much the property will appreciate over the next twenty-five years. Although we can't be sure, the past is a prologue and can reasonably be used to make an estimate.

The example property increased in value over the span of twenty-five years from $179,500 to $729,500. That increase of $550,000 represents an annual increase in value of 5.75 percent. I'll use the same parameters as I used before, but to be conservative, I will lower the appreciation rate to just 5 percent. Even so, here is how that property value will look twenty-five years down the road:

| | |
|---|---|
| Market Value | $2,470,000 |

During my career, I have found that when I do projections far into the future my clients get skeptical about the numbers, especially if they are new to real estate investing. This still seems to be the case even when I present statistics from the past.

Having said that, I wanted to show you what this four-unit building might do cash flow-wise twenty-five years from now. I'll assume you paid the loan off in that period. In addition, I will increase the current income 3 percent per year and the expenses 2 percent per year.

| | |
|---|---|
| Monthly Income | $10,050 |
| Monthly Expenses | $2,362 |
| Projected Cash Flow | $7,688 |

Why is real estate such a smart retirement investment? Perhaps Mark Twain understood the Appreciation Game better than anyone when he declared, "Buy land. They're not making it anymore."

## YOUR YELLOW BRICK ROAD

Now that you are aware of how appreciation really works, let's lay the groundwork for making it happen for you.

There is no way any of us can become experts in all the areas of life that affect us, but on the really important issues— the ones that hit us in the pocketbook— it is incumbent that we develop a good basic understanding of how they work. Here's a simple question: How many of us have an incredible base of knowledge about sports or our favorite movie star's life but don't know what the LIBOR is? Exactly. LIBOR is the London Interbank Offered Rate.

I am not poking fun at anyone for having fun. Actually being able to enjoy life to the fullest is one of the biggest benefits to finally taking charge of your future. What I have seen is that most of us tend to abdicate all responsibility for our future to the professionals we hire to help us, not unlike an ostrich that buries its head in the sand at the first sign of trouble. Of course you need an educated stockbroker to help pick the right stocks or a trained real estate professional to help choose which property to buy, but wouldn't it be nice if you had a keen understanding of either of those fields before you hired someone else to run the ship?

I also know that most of us are impatient. Once we read a book on this or take a course on that and the light bulb goes on, well, we can't wait to get started. To this, I say, "Wait!" People have and will continue to make fortunes investing in all kinds of investments, including real estate. Opportunities to make money are not going to go away. I say be patient. Take the time to gain the basic knowledge necessary, so you can make sound decisions on what to invest in and who to turn to for help. Remember, investing doesn't guarantee a return, but knowledge certainly helps make the odds much more attractive.

You can educate yourself, utilize some sound business principles, and then implement an ultraconservative investment plan and take much of the risk out of real estate investing while still allowing for a sizable return on your investment. In the end, you'll have created a yellow brick road to your own retirement. If you're interested, I have a plan to help.

## THE THREE-POINT PLAN

My plan is fairly simple and designed to keep you in the game for as long as you have your money invested. This isn't meant to be "Real Estate Investing 101," which you take once and forget. This is more like a continuing education class, one that you should be involved in for the rest of your investment career. Just as you educated yourself for that day job, I want you to educate yourself for this investment career. You work at your day job and trade your time for dollars.

In your investment career, you will be letting your investments do most of the work, but you need to be the brains of the operation. Yes, you will be hiring some experts to help, but it takes knowledge to hire the right people.

The three key steps of a plan for success are:

1. learn;
2. plan; and
3. invest.

Let's touch on each of these components.

## STEP ONE: LEARN

The first step, learning, can be the toughest for most of us because learning anything new requires lots of personal effort. When it comes to full-time careers, if you wanted to be an engineer, you would go to college and get a degree in engineering. But, don't worry, a formal education is not necessary for you to learn what you need to learn in order to succeed in real estate investing.

Thankfully, thousands of books, articles, classes, seminars, and recordings are available on most investment subjects. Even better news is that most of the books, articles, and some of the recordings probably will be available for free at the local library. To supplement your independent study, plenty of colleges and adult education schools offer courses on everything from basic accounting to property management. Most are informative and reasonably priced.

For the majority of us, finding the time to devote to a new venture is one of the toughest problems we face. I have found that many audio programs are available on a host of investment subjects, not just real estate. They can be tougher to locate, but they are worth the effort. You can literally turn your daily commute into an education effort by using the time to listen to these audio educational programs rather than talk radio or music. It would be a trade-off, but one that could get you that much closer to catching the golden goose.

An important part of learning is researching the local market. Like test-driving a car before you buy, you will begin using what you've learned about your investment vehicle in the real world. In real estate, you will learn about capitalization rates, gross multipliers, and the price per square foot as ways of comparing properties. These rates can vary greatly even in the same city. Once you understand these concepts and their importance, you can begin to get a feeling for the statistics on the properties in your area.

You can actually begin the research phase of this plan while you are learning about investing in general. You don't need a four-year college education to be able to get a gut-level feeling about the products you're researching. Just as you can research various no-load mutual funds that are growth-oriented, you can discover what duplexes are selling for in your neighborhood. During this process you should also begin to research the experts in the field, so you will ultimately find the professionals you will feel comfortable with and have confidence in. Feel free to meet with real estate agents and loan brokers. Interview them as if you're considering hiring them for a job—because you are.

A word of warning: did you ever hear the phrase "a little knowledge is a dangerous thing"? Well, by this point, you will have a little knowledge and it will indeed be a dangerous thing. By diving in and doing the kind of research I'm recommending, you will probably be enthusiastic about getting started. You will start seeing "good deals" out there and be tempted to jump in right away. But put the brakes on! Wait at least until you complete step two in this process, the planning phase. This way you will have a self-written road map to help guide you toward your dreams.

## STEP TWO: PLAN

Planning is the key to being successful in any business. Certainly, knowledge and research are important, but if you strike out spending your money on the wrong products, you may not reach your goals. A great buy on a duplex that produces no cash flow does little for a retired investor who needs income.

Later, we will be reviewing planning in detail. But, in short, a good plan starts with defining what your goals are. Your goal cannot be to find a "good deal." When it comes to investing, everyone's goal is to find one of those; that's a given in the field. When you tell your real estate agent that you're looking for a "good deal," it lets him or her know how little you really are in touch with your true needs.

The previous exercise to determine your lump-sum gap and the amount to fund your dreams was designed to help you focus on measurable goals from your investments. These should be the things you want for you and your family. These become flags on your financial road map to keep you on course to reaching your goals. It is chasing the truly important personal things that make life a wonderful experience. Don't get caught at the end of your life realizing you were using someone else's map.

## STEP THREE: INVEST

The third step in the plan is where you make your move. This is when you get to put that knowledge and research to work by investing and buying your first property. This is where the real work starts because it's not just a mind game now; it's for real.

When you've finally decided it's time to buy something, take a deep breath and review all you've learned and researched before you make that first purchase. This can be as exciting as buying your first car or home, so the deep breath will save you from jumping for the first property that seems to be "exactly" what you want. Remember what Will Rogers said: "Don't just grab the first thing that comes by. Know what to turn down."

When you get to the point of actually making an investment, the process can take a while. This is especially true when purchasing a piece of real estate. But if that looking-around time seems to go on way too long, you may have to reassess the standards and goals in your plan. Remember, you can analyze, research, and plan until you're blue in the face, but it's impossible to make a profit investing in real estate if you don't actually make an investment. What's more, it's pretty easy in the textbook world of learning and research to be out of step with the real world. Make sure you ask your expert to let you know if your goals are out of line with the current market. In the end, make a purchase and get started.

Owning property is like going to work after you are finished with school. We all have heard the story of the person who started in the mail room and ended up running the entire company. Well, in real estate you don't have to begin with a twenty-unit building to be successful. You can start small too. How about purchasing a modest duplex close to where you live? Or, better yet, if you don't own a home yet, buy a duplex and live in one of the units. That's what we call "starting in the mail room" of the real estate business. It is a nice, safe, conservative approach.

When you own property, you have the full responsibility of running it. However, just as surgeons don't perform operations before they are properly trained, neither should you invest a penny until you are trained. Chapter nine is devoted to this topic, but let's hit some highlights now.

Once you are trained, the good news is you will own the property and you can do as much or as little of the work as you like. You are in charge of the property, the rents, and the tenants. In good times you can hire out most of the work, and in the tough times you can do it yourself. You are in control.

You have to work at it and assume the responsibility, but that's what makes it safe for you.

You've got a day job that you call a career, but you're just trading time for dollars there. Now, whether you've hung a shingle or not, you are heading up your own real estate company as the CEO and CFO all rolled into one. You're in charge of investing your hard-earned money, and the success of this operation depends solely on you and how well you do the job. This is frightening, but liberating at the same time.

Take another deep breath. Remember, you've conducted your research, you've studied the market, and you've planned where you're going. As I've said before, this isn't a get-rich-quick program. You are on a life journey. The plan is to invest your money to grow your net worth to meet the goals you have set for you and your family.

You will find that if you are doing your job right as the manager, you will be constantly revisiting the first steps of the plan for success. As you manage, you learn—not from books but from actually doing the job.

Along the way you will take the time to assess the current market and compare your position with the goals of your plan. At some point as head of this company, you will decide that it's time to trade up or refinance. Either way, you may realize that the time is ripe to acquire more property and you are going to use your currently owned buildings to help you do it. The fun is just beginning!

—— $ ——

"I was introduced to Marty Stone soon after I had exited a high-paying career in the film biz. I was wondering how I was going to make a living. When I met him, we had meetings and he became very aware of who I was and what my needs were. Through our conversations, I learned his concepts about building wealth through real estate. I come from a solid family of real estate and stock investors. I completely aligned with Marty's steadfast vision for building a portfolio. Nothing fancy or quick or aggressive. It was about acquiring properties, fixing them up as needed, raising rents, and then taking your equity and buying another building by either refinancing or doing an exchange up into a bigger building, thus expanding your capacity to make even more money from the initial investment. It's really simple. He taught me how to let the economic forces that affected real estate do most of the wealth creation.

"After only six years, I quit working at age forty-two and started living a life people dream about. I own a home on the beach in Mexico and also own a 180-degree ocean-view house in Laguna Beach, California. It has now been fifteen years since starting with Marty. My income and net worth are in the stratosphere. I had no idea how powerful this would be. My $500k initial investment is now a $12 million portfolio! Projections are that it will double every ten years. I am thankful every day!"

—*Leslie S.*

—— CRITICAL CONCEPT ——

## Inflation

The major component of appreciation is inflation. "Inflation" is the term that describes the fact that our money is losing its purchasing power, so we need to bring more dollars to buy something today as compared to what we had to pay a few years ago. I like to talk about gas because we've been using it for a long time. When I was in college, gas was about twenty cents per gallon. Today, they charge $3.75 per gallon. The same thing happens to the price of property, regardless of what property you buy.

Real estate does have one more component, and that is demand. In many areas of the country, there is more "demand" for property than there is "available inventory" or supply in the market, so the prices get bid up by the people trying to buy or rent. If you want to see how demand affects prices, find the cost of a piece of property from twenty to thirty years ago in an area you know and then find its current value. If you go to www.usinflationcalculator.com, you will be able to put the value in the calculator and the number of years (twenty to thirty) and it will adjust the current pricing for the effects of inflation. If the real value today is above that number, then that extra cost is an effect of the additional demand.

# 4

# Components of Return

*"Money is better than poverty, if only for financial reasons."*
—Woody Allen

When investing in residential real estate, these components of return will help you reach your goals:

1. Cash flow

2. Loan reduction

3. Appreciation

4. Tax benefits

To take full advantage of real estate as an investment, all four components of return must be factored into the equation. In this chapter, you will learn about each component independently and then how to calculate the combined effect of each of them to produce an anticipated overall return on your investment. For consistency, I will discuss the four-unit property introduced in the previous chapter.

## CASH FLOW

The first component of return and the one that usually gets the most attention from novice investors is cash flow. In simple terms, cash flow is the money you get to keep after all the expenses have been paid. The misnomer made by many beginning investors is that cash flow is the component of return that helps you grow wealthy. True, it's nice to be on the positive side at the end of each month, but when it comes to true wealth building, it's the other components that really do the trick.

Nonetheless, to determine cash flow, you need to know the following:

1. Annual gross income

2. Annual expenses

3. Total debt payment on your loans

## INCOME

There are three ways to look at the income a building produces. The first way is by examining the scheduled rent. Scheduled rent is the sum total of all the established rents for the building. This analysis assumes that each tenant is paying in full and that there are no vacancies.

The second way to look at the income is by analyzing the potential rent. Potential rent is the income you can earn if you were charging market rent for your building. This analysis is based on the rents that other property owners in your neighborhood are receiving. This is where any ongoing rental income research you do can have a major impact on your cash flow and, in later years, on the ultimate value of your property.

The most effective way to analyze the income on a building is to look at the collected rent. A collected rent analysis is like swearing before a judge; it tells the truth, the whole truth, and nothing but the truth. This analysis tells what money was actually taken in over a period of time. It combines the rent that was collected as well as the rent that was not, plus adds in the true cost for any vacancies that occurred.

Note that the credit losses you endure from bad debts will depend on a few things: the general state of the economy, the economic level of your tenant base and, most important, your adeptness as an effective property manager. Remember, however, credit losses from occasional vacancies are par for the course in this business and come with the territory. In the very best scenario, your vacancies would only be "turnovers" (a change of tenants with no lost rent). This goal often can be achieved but will require hands-on management on your part.

## EXPENSES

Expenses are the second factor in determining cash flow on a piece of real estate. There are three different types of expenses: fixed expenses, variable expenses, and capital expenses.

Fixed expenses are the commonplace recurring costs required when holding a property, including insurance premiums, property taxes, and city business license fees. They are called "fixed expenses" because the amount you pay on a regular basis does not change.

Variable expenses, on the other hand, do change. These expenses are all the other costs you may incur while managing your rental property, including general upkeep, maintenance, and utility payments. Obviously, the effective management of variable expenses will play a pivotal role in how much cash flow a building produces.

The last type is capital expenses. Capital expenses are defined as major items that have a useful life of more than one year, like a new driveway, a new roof, or exterior paint. For tax purposes, these items must be capitalized or written off over a period of years. To account for capital expenses in your cash flow, you will need to include a reserve (a certain percentage of the income based on the condition of the property).

## CASH FLOW

Now we'll calculate cash flow for our example property. Here we have four units that rent for a total of $4,800 per month. Multiply $4,800 by twelve months and the gross scheduled income on the property is $57,600 per year. Furthermore, the actual annual expenses add up to $17,280 and the loan payment is $2,691 per month, which is $32,292 yearly.

We put down \$182,500 to buy the property, so we can compute our cash flow return as follows:

| Gross Annual Income | \$57,600 |
|---|---|
| Less Operating Expenses | – \$17,280 |
| Less Annual Loan Payments | – \$32,292 |
| Annual Cash Flow | \$ 8,028 |

Our goal wasn't cash-on-cash return. If it was, we would have made a much more significant down payment. Rather, our goal was to start investing now to ensure a cash flow for retirement.

## LOAN REDUCTION

Loan reduction is the second way your equity will grow over the tenure of your purchase. When you close on a piece of real estate, your initial equity is your down payment. Thankfully, with the help of your tenants, your equity will dramatically increase over the years. This is because you are making monthly payments on your mortgage using tenant income. In the first few years of ownership, it's difficult to notice loan reduction as much of a return because so much of your payment is going toward interest. But in latter years, your monthly mortgage payments pay down principal at a rapid rate, which significantly increases your equity.

To illustrate equity growth from loan reduction, let's return to our four-unit example property. To recap, we financed a $547,000 loan that was payable at $2,691 per month. The payment included interest at 4.25 percent per year as well as principal reduction. The total payments on the loan for the year are $32,292. Given these facts, we can compute our equity growth returns in the first year as follows:

| | |
|---|---|
| Total Loan Payments | $32,292 |
| Less Interest Paid | –$23,248 |
| Principal Reduction | $ 9,044 |

The third way your equity grows is through value appreciation. Value appreciation results from two factors: inflation and demand. Inflationary appreciation sounds like what it is—the increase in a piece of real estate's value caused by inflation. This appreciation rate is directly linked to the general inflationary rate of the country's overall economy. When the country's inflation rate is up, the appreciation rate of property usually is also up.

Demand is the second factor connected to appreciation. Demand appreciation is related to four economic principles. They are:

1. scarcity;
2. transferability;
3. utility; and
4. demand.

These four components can affect a property's appreciation rate in varying degrees. It is the combined effect of these principles that pushes property values up at a greater rate in some areas while pushing values down in others.

The scarcity principle can best be seen when comparing an urban area to a rural one. In urban areas, it is nearly impossible to find any undeveloped land. Just think of New York City or downtown Chicago, and you'll get the picture. In cities like these, to build a new building, an existing older building must be bulldozed. Therefore, you first must find someone willing to sell. Once that is accomplished, you'll most definitely be paying a premium for both the land and the existing structure that sits on it. Naturally, this drives prices up. Rural areas, on the other hand, tend to have plenty of vacant land available. This greater availability of land makes it pretty simple to find willing sellers, and the end result is lower prices for real estate.

Transferability refers to the ease of buying and selling any commodity. As you know, investments such as stocks and bonds are fairly liquid because you can transfer them from one owner to another pretty quickly. Real estate, on the other hand, can't trade hands nearly so fast. This is usually related to the number of potential buyers and the ability or lack thereof to find adequate financing. There may be many buyers and hundreds of lenders for the modest two-bedroom, one-bath home you are trying to sell, but how many buyers and lenders would be interested or qualified to buy the Chrysler Building? Significantly fewer.

Utility refers to the usability of property. With real estate, the value of a property is directly related to its highest and best use. For example, a small parcel of land in a residential area will probably be limited by the potential value of the home that can be built on it. A large commercial lot close to a highway entrance or a shipyard, however, could be an extremely valuable location to build a manufacturing plant. According to this principle, the greater the utility value, the greater the price of the property.

Finally, the demand principle of appreciation results from the upward desirability of the property. This is the same phenomenon that affects the price of tickets to any major event that sells out at a moment's notice. Think about the scalpers who roam the parking lot of the Super Bowl or a Bruce Springsteen concert. The reason they are able to get top dollar for their tickets is because the demand for their product is great. If these scalpers were hawking tickets to see a clown making balloon animals, odds are they wouldn't attract many top-dollar buyers.

General trends in the economy also play a significant role in changes in demand. Many investors move from one investment vehicle to another based on the investment's ability to produce a buck. When stocks are up, their money is there. When bond yields increase, the stocks are sold for bonds. When real estate is moving, they start buying. This sends the message to all the small investors that it is time to buy. The end result is an increased demand for a product that is in limited supply. In times like these, appreciation rates naturally increase.

To give an example of how appreciation affects price, let's make an estimate using our example property.

Remember, we bought it for $729,500. We'll assume the appreciation rate is 5 percent per year. At that price and with that appreciation rate, the return looks like this:

| | |
|---|---:|
| Price of Property | $729,500 |
| Appreciation Rate | × 5% |
| Total Return | $ 36,475 |

## TAX BENEFITS

The fourth and final component of return is tax-sheltered benefits. These are the paper losses you can deduct from the taxable income you receive from the property. Because you are the owner of an investment property, the Internal Revenue Service (IRS) allots you an annual depreciation allowance to deduct against your income. The premise is this deduction will be saved up and used to replace the property at the end of its useful life. For most businesses, this is a necessary deduction because equipment like fax machines and computers wear out after time. But when it comes to real estate, most property owners don't live long enough or keep their buildings long enough for them to wear out. Therefore, the tax savings from the deduction is a profit that is added to your overall financial return.

There are a few different methods you can use to determine your annual depreciation allowance. The most common method relies on using the land-to-improvement ratios found on your property tax bill. Don't be concerned if the actual dollar amount shown on the tax bill doesn't match what you're paying for the property; it is the ratio we are looking for. The idea is to use the ratio numbers to get the percentage you need to determine the value of the improvements. To do this, use the following calculation:

Assessed Improvement Value ÷ Total Assessed Value
= % Value of Improvements

Once you know the percentage value of improvements, you then multiply that by the sales price to get the amount of depreciable improvements:

% Value of Improvements × Price
= Depreciable Improvements

Keep in mind that you don't have to establish your depreciation schedule until you file your tax return. In most cases, there will usually be sufficient time between the property closing and the tax filing deadline to discuss the method you want to use with your tax professional.

## MODIFIED ACCELERATED COST RECOVERY SYSTEM (MACRS)

As of the writing of this book, we do not have a clear understanding of how the tax code changes just passed by Congress will play out over time. It appears that the depreciation periods for many components of investment property will be lowered, which will increase the tax deductions. Check with your certified public accountant to see the actual new rules as the new tax code becomes available. The tax code change in 1986 established the Modified Accelerated Cost Recovery System (MACRS). This code established the recovery period or useful life of assets to be depreciated. Like much of the government's tax code, these periods usually bear no correlation to the useful life of an asset. Nonetheless, in the case of improved property, there are two classes of property and two recovery periods that were established. They are:

| Type of Property | Recovery Period/Useful Life |
| --- | --- |
| Residential | 27.5 years |
| Nonresidential | 39 years |

Note that it doesn't matter what the true age of your property is. If your property is residential, you use 27.5 years. If your property is categorized as nonresidential, you use 39 years. Additionally, when using this method of depreciation, you will have the same amount of annual depreciation expense over the entire useful life of the building. To arrive at the annual expense, you simply divide the value of the depreciable improvements by the recovery period, which gives you your deduction.

Now let's take a look at the calculation using the example property. First, we find the value of improvements and then divide that value by the recovery period. We are paying $729,500 for the property and are using the land and improvement ratios from the tax bill as described earlier.

The tax bill shows the improvements assessed at $325,000 and the total assessed value of the property at $434,000. We would then calculate the depreciation allowance as follows:

$325,000 Improvements ÷ $434,000 Total Assessed Value
= 75% Improvements

We would then multiply the sales price by the improvement percentage to get the amount of depreciable improvements:

$729,500 × 75% = $549,500 Depreciable Improvements

Finally, to determine our annual appreciation allowance, we divide the depreciable improvements by the recovery period:

$549,500 ÷ 27.5 = $19,982 Annual Depreciation Allowance

Before we can determine what kind of savings our depreciation allowance gives us, we first need to review two other code changes made in the tax reform of 1986. They are important because these changes limit your ability to use the excess depreciation to shelter the income from your other job.

The first new code change classifies real estate investors into either "active" or "passive" investors. Passive investors are defined as those who buy property as limited partners or with a group of more than ten other partners. As a passive investor, you can use the depreciation deduction to shelter any profit from the property. Any excess write-off must be carried forward to be used as the profit from the building increases. The theory is this money is like having a savings account of tax benefits that can be drawn on to cover future profits.

An active investor is one who buys the property alone or with just a couple of partners who are "materially participating" in the management of the building. You actively participate in your real estate if you make management decisions or arrange for others to provide these services in a significant bona fide sense. These decisions might include approving new tenants, setting rental rates and terms, approving expenditures, and any other decisions that might have to do with running the property. Even if you have hired management to care for day-to-day operations, you materially participate in the property and are an "active investor," according to the IRS, if the buck stops with you.

Additionally, the IRS has categorized investors into two different types:

1. Those who consider real estate investing and management as their primary career.

2. Those who invest in real estate in addition to their regular career.

In the Revenue Reconciliation Act of 1993, Congress relaxed the rules somewhat for the active real estate investor. The act allowed taxpayers who met the requirements necessary to be considered a real estate professional to bypass the passive activity rules for real estate investments in which they materially participated. In other words, an active real estate investor could now apply unlimited losses from their real estate activities against any other earned income.

The IRS defines a "real estate professional" as follows:

- a taxpayer who performs in excess of 750 hours of personal services during the tax year in real property trades and business, and

- over half of her/his personal services performed during the year were in real property trades and businesses.

Most investors fall into the category in which real estate is something they do in addition to their regular career. If this describes you, then your real estate losses will be limited to $25,000. For example, your adjusted gross income before real estate deductions is $50,000 and your losses from property are $30,000. In this scenario, you would only be able to deduct $25,000 of the $30,000. But don't fret; you don't lose the remaining $5,000. Instead, it would go into that tax-sheltered bank account mentioned earlier. What this deduction means is that instead of paying tax on $50,000 of income, you pay tax only on $25,000. And because the tax you save is a profit, it is therefore included in the overall return from your investment.

From a realistic perspective, assuming your properties run at a break-even cash flow or better, this threshold of $25,000 takes a long time to reach. In fact, with the MACRS depreciation and an improvement ratio of 70 percent, you would have to own almost $1,000,000 worth of property to reach $25,000 of excess depreciation. As your properties become more profitable, you can use more of the depreciation to shelter the property income and have less to shelter your regular career income.

Another code change from the Tax Reform Act of 1986 limits your ability to use the losses from your real estate against the earnings from your regular career. This limit applies when your earnings exceed $100,000, after which you will lose $1 of deduction for every $2 you earn over $100,000. This would mean that at $150,000 you would have no deduction against your income. But remember, these are not lost; they are just saved for future use.

Now, knowing all that, let's go back to our four-unit example and calculate your tax benefit. We will assume you are an active investor in the 28 percent federal tax bracket. To calculate your tax savings, we need to first shelter the taxable profit from the property. As you will recall, you have a taxable cash flow of $8,028 and a taxable equity growth from loan reduction of $9,044 per year. We calculate the carryover loss as follows:

| | |
|---|---|
| Depreciation Allowance | $19,982 |
| Less Cash Flow | – $ 8,028 |
| Less Equity Growth | – $ 9,044 |
| Tax-Sheltered Benefit | $ 2,910 |

The tax savings is calculated by multiplying the tax bracket by the sheltered benefit:

| | |
|---|---|
| Tax-Sheltered Benefit | $2,910 |
| Tax Rate | × 28% |
| Tax Savings | $ 815 |

Besides federal taxes, many states require you to pay state income tax. Their rules are usually similar to the federal rules when it comes to deductions and depreciation. If you live in a state with a tax, you will receive additional savings and you can use this same formula to estimate those figures.

## PUTTING IT ALL TOGETHER

Now let's look at the total annual tax-deferred return combining all four components. You have a cash flow of $8,028, equity growth from loan reduction of $9,044, equity growth from appreciation of $36,475, and tax savings of $815. The calculation looks like this:

| | |
|---|---|
| Cash Flow | $ 8,028 |
| Loan Reduction | $ 9,044 |
| Appreciation | $36,475 |
| Tax Savings | + $  815 |
| Total Return | $54,362 |

Because the down payment was $182,500 to purchase the property, we can compute the total return as follows:

Total Return $54,362 ÷ Down Payment $182,500
= 29.7% Return on Investment

Figure 4.1 is a basic worksheet to help you calculate the returns. All you need is a calculator.

FIGURE 4.1

## PROPERTY ANALYSIS WORKSHEET

Address: Basic Return

1. Value of Property                                        _____
2. Loans on Property                                       _____
3. Equity in Property (Line 2 – Line 3)
4. Gross Income _____ Month x 12 =        _____
5. Expenses        _____ Month x 12 =        _____
6. Loan Payments _____ Month x 12 =     _____
7. Interest ( _____ Loan Amount x _____ %) =   _____
8. Loan Payoff (Line 6 – Line 7) =                     _____
9. Cash Flow (Line 4 – Line 5 – Line 6) =          _____
10. Depreciation Deduction                             _____
11. Tax Shelter (Line 10 – Line 9 – Line 8)          _____
12. Tax Savings (Tax Bracket _____ % x Line 11) = _____
13. Building Profit (Line 8 + Line 9 + Line 12) = _____
14. Basic Return (Line 13 ÷ Line 3) =                _____

Return on Equity
15. Cash Flow (Line 9)                                      _____
16. Loan Payoff (Line 8)                                   _____
17. Tax Savings (Line 12)                                 _____
18. Appreciation _____ % x Line 1                 _____
19. Total Investment Return
    (Lines 15 + 16 + 17 + 18)                            _____
20. Return on Equity (Line 19 ÷ Line 3)            _____

To save some arithmetic, there are many computer-generated systems for calculating this return. Some are proprietary systems written by their firms, and many are just modified spreadsheet systems. If you have access to one of these systems, it will save time. But having an automated system is not necessary.

"I was working as a writer and had some investments in the stock market, but after the debacle with WorldCom and Enron, I felt uncomfortable banking on Wall Street. I am cautious by nature and was very worried about trying something new, but Marty's strategy gave me the confidence to buy my first apartment building. I was able to expand my portfolio, and now I have nine properties—all of them cash flow positive. Several of them are almost fully paid off since I financed a handful with fifteen-year fixed loans. My friends who stayed in the stock market have watched their fortunes ebb and flow, while I have been able to steadily build wealth and security, and know beyond a shadow of a doubt that I will be leaving my two children not only a great start in life but a pathway to smart investing."

—*Efrem S.*

# ——— CRITICAL CONCEPT ———
## Using OPM to Create Wealth

So what's OPM? It's Other People's Money. But a better term is "leverage." Leverage allows you to make a better return on the money you invest because instead of paying cash for the investment, you borrow most of the cost of the investment. To give you a basic idea, consider the facts I used earlier about a gallon of gas. When the gallon was twenty cents, if I had been able to buy four gallons using my twenty cents as a down payment and borrowing sixty cents, here is where I would be today.

I could sell the four gallons for $3.75 each, for a total of $15.00. I could then pay off my sixty-cent loan and pay myself back the twenty cents, so my net profit would be $14.20. That is a great return on my original twenty cents. There are more expenses related to using leverage, but the point is it can significantly raise the profit on the capital you have.

# 5

# Your Winning Lottery Ticket

*"Long-range planning does not deal with future decisions but with the future of present decisions."*

—Peter Drucker, Author

As you've noticed by now, my approach to real estate investing is pretty conservative. I've based our example property not on helping you get rich but rather on trying to give you insight into how a relatively small real estate purchase now could fund a safe and plentiful life for you later. In fact, securing that kind of trouble-free peace of mind is the primary reason so many Americans play the lottery week after week. I'll show you specifically why investing in real estate is akin to winning your own lottery and, second, how to plan ahead so the numbers you choose will come in.

## YOUR WINNING NUMBERS

In the real world, it's no secret that it takes money to make money. If you don't have any money to invest, it's going to be tough to make a profit. That's probably why the lottery is so popular; it gives anyone with a buck a chance to be a millionaire. We don't have the magic solution for everyone. However, if you can manage to save just enough to get started investing, at least you'll give yourself a fighting chance at retirement.

## SHARING THE SECRETS

Albert Einstein was once asked what the most powerful force in the universe was. Without hesitation, he answered, "Compound interest." Years before, Ben Franklin called compound interest "the stone that will turn lead into gold." Combine compound interest with leverage and you get the two components that launch real estate investing into a stratosphere all its own.

Whether we know it or not, compound interest is a fairly well-known principle. If you put money in the bank, the bankers refer to the amount of money you will earn in terms of the "yield." Your yield will be higher than the interest rate quoted on your account. This is because the bank assumes you will be leaving the profit (interest) in the bank along with the original amount you invested. The idea is you will earn interest on the interest. In the end, this process raises the amount you earn on your original investment by leaps and bounds.

A math lesson might help. Here is the formula for calculating how much compound interest will increase your return:

$$FV = PV(1 + I)^n$$

Don't panic! This math isn't as overwhelming as it looks. What's more, most calculators have this formula built in, so it's a snap for the average person to work out. Nonetheless, so you can impress your family and friends, the components of the compound interest algorithm translate this way:

- FV = **F**uture **V**alue of the investment you make

- PV = **P**resent **V**alue of that investment

- I = Average **I**nterest rate you earn on the investment

- n = **N**umber of years you keep your money invested

Simply, this formula will give you an estimate of what the money you have today (PV) will be worth in the future (FV). This estimate is based on the percentage you earn (I) over the years (n) you have your money invested.

For example, if you had $10,000 to invest and could earn just 5 percent on it for the next twenty to twenty-five years, here's how your money would grow because of the effects of compound interest.

$10,000 @ 5% for 20 years = $26,533
$10,000 @ 5% for 25 years = $33,863

Pretty nice, isn't it? But the story gets even better. To see the real advantage to real estate investing, we need to add the second wealth-building concept into this equation: leverage. According to Merriam-Webster, *leverage* is defined as "an increased means of accomplishing some purpose." When it comes to investing, our definition is "making money using someone else's money."

What's great is the entire real estate industry is built around encouraging the use of other people's money to fund these types of investments. The biggest proponent of the concept is the federal government via the Federal Housing Administration (FHA) and the Department of Veterans Affairs (VA). The FHA and VA encourage home ownership by offering financing for home buyers with low or no down payment programs. The purpose is to encourage people to own their own homes. These FHA and VA loans are nothing more than loans designed to take advantage of leverage, which is encouraged by our government.

What's amazing is so many people take advantage of using borrowed money to buy a home but never take advantage of this idea to make any additional real estate investments that could secure their future for good. These same homeowners marvel at how much their home appreciates over the years, but when it comes to long-term planning, this light bulb always stays dim. So let's get out of the dark.

As you learned, one of the great advantages of real estate is it offers several types of return. The cash flow gives you something to spend today, yet the appreciation creates the big-time wealth for your future via the use of leverage. To demonstrate the effect of leverage, let's talk about just this one component of return from real estate: value appreciation.

The value of property increases in most areas of the country because of inflation and demand. Bread, milk, and gas seem to cost more every year and, thankfully for real estate investors, so does housing. We call that value appreciation. Appreciation rates vary all over the country, but regardless of where you live, most areas always seem to have some steady increase in value as the years go on. To demonstrate how this will work to your benefit, we'll use a rate of 5 percent appreciation for the following example. If you own a property worth $500,000, this means that it will go up 5 percent in price every year. If you paid all cash for your house, this means you earn 5 percent on your $500,000, which is $25,000.

Paying all cash for a property, however, isn't what makes real estate investors money. Rather, it's using leverage to its full advantage that creates their real wealth. The idea is to use a little bit of your own money, lots of someone else's, and then reap the rewards of 100 percent of the investment. Here's an illustration of a return after one year of ownership assuming two different down payment options. We'll use a 20 percent down payment (the amount it would take with a conventional loan) and a 3 percent down payment (offered on many properties through FHA) and factor in the same modest 5 percent appreciation rate as before. Here is what is possible:

| Down Payment | Appreciation | Percentage Return on Down Payment |
|---|---|---|
| $100,000 | $25,000 | 25% |
| $15,000 | $25,000 | 167% |

A return of 167 percent isn't anything to scoff at, especially when you compare it to the meager returns you can get on your money at the bank or credit union. Even the 25 percent return from the 20 percent down payment scenario looks great compared to most other investments. And, remember, value appreciation is only one component of return from an investment in real estate. This investment, as you know, will help you make money three other ways (cash flow, loan reduction, and tax benefits), and it's the combination of all the returns that creates the kind of money needed to fund a retirement worth smiling about.

For the pièce de résistance, let's work that compound interest formula again by adding leverage (your money + the borrowed money) into the mix. Even though our example showed a 25 percent return from appreciation alone, we will be ultraconservative and scale back to a 20 percent return.

$100,000 @ 20% for 20 years = $3,833,760
$100,000 @ 20% for 25 years = $9,539,622

Yes, you read those numbers right. Amazing isn't it? Though we used the same $100,000 initial investment, our return this time shot through the roof! In fact, so much so that you could fund a pretty great future on those kinds of figures—all due to using compound interest and its best friend, leverage.

Now that you can see how to hit the lottery, let's learn how to put together a plan so you can actually do it for yourself.

## COMPONENTS OF YOUR PLAN

Although good investment plans do not start out in minute detail, you should put your ideas down on paper from day one. To get things started, buy yourself a sturdy three-ring binder to put your plan in. This way, you can change the contents easily as you make purchases and progress over the years. Divide your planning binder into the following four sections:

1. Goals
2. General Plan
3. Detailed Plan
4. Follow-up and Goal Review

In the remainder of this chapter, I will go over each of these sections of your plan in detail.

## GOALS

This section of your plan is its lifeblood. Here you will lay out your long-term investment goals and the time frame you have scheduled for their achievement. The goals section of your investment plan should be divided into the following five subsections:

1. Cash-flow requirements

2. Net-worth projections

3. Tax-sheltered benefits required

4. Cash withdrawal from plan

5. Other goals

Let's look at each of these subsections one at a time.

**Cash-Flow Requirements.** The cash-flow requirements refer to your cash-flow projections during and after completion of the plan. If you make enough money at your day job, you may not need any cash flow from your real estate. If so, that would be great because you'll be able to plow any cash flow you create right back into your buildings. On the other hand, a little bit of extra cash each month might be just what you need. Your retirement fund will suffer a bit, but your day-to-day existence will be all the better for it.

The point at which you will begin to achieve a significant cash flow depends on two things:

1. The initial amount of cash you invest in the plan

2. How well you manage your plan

Cash flow is generated from a property in two ways. The first is by looking at what remains after you pay all the expenses and outstanding loans each month. This cash flow should increase yearly as you increase rents. By the time you retire, this cash flow can be considerable, depending on the amount of financing you have left on your buildings.

The second source of cash flow comes from the eventual sale of the building and carrying your equity as a note against the property. As a general rule, the cash flow at that time will be equal to the going rate of interest multiplied by the net equity of your property. For many retirees, selling their buildings and carrying some (or all) of the paper will give them a much higher return on their nest eggs as compared to the typical savings account, certificate of deposit, or other investment.

Another benefit is that by carrying the financing on a property, you postpone the capital gains taxes due. Uncle Sam says that as long as you're receiving interest only and not getting any principal payments, your capital gains tax will be postponed because the government considers this an installment sale.

**Your Future Net Worth.** Your net-worth projection is the amount of money you want to be worth at the end of a given period of time. If your lump-sum gap from chapter two showed that you were $500,000 short for retirement, your net-worth projection might look like this:

> "Attain a net worth of $500,000 for retirement
> at the end of a fifteen-year real estate investment
> plan."

As I have shown, net worth and cash flow are related. In cases where your investment plan is set up as a retirement vehicle, your net-worth projections will probably be ten to twelve times your net annual cash-flow requirements. This assumes that at the time of retirement you will be able to locate savings investments that offer yields of from 8 to 10 percent per annum. Based on the available returns for the past ten to twenty years, this is a pretty reasonable assumption.

You may wish to set your net-worth projections for reasons other than just cash-flow requirements. Remember all the extras we thought up at the end of chapter two, such as cabins, boats, and college tuition for grandchildren? This is where you declare those things will happen—by factoring the necessary money into your projection. By putting it down on paper today, you'll set the stage for it to come true tomorrow.

**Tax Benefits.** In this section of your planning binder, you should write out what kinds of tax benefits you plan to achieve. Tax-sheltered benefits in real estate investments are complicated and can vary widely. Therefore, I have devoted an entire chapter later in this book to this subject. For now, I will provide a few necessary guidelines for you to keep in mind:

- I don't recommend that you buy real estate for tax benefits only. Even though there are lots of great tax advantages to owning investment real estate, many of them have been diluted with the tax law changes in the late 1980s. Effects of the tax law of 2018 are still to be determined.

- It is important to consider the amount of depreciable improvements when making your final decision on which building to purchase. Remember that the property with the highest land-to-improvement ratio will give you the highest write-off and, thus, the best return.

- If necessary, consider using installment sales to create cash flow during the life of your plan.

- Use 1031 tax-deferred exchanges to grow your nest egg.

Given these guidelines, a reasonable tax goal might be as follows:

"Maximize tax benefits on real estate purchases and use 1031 tax-deferred exchange and installment sales when available."

**Cash Withdrawal.** It's important to plan in advance for periods when you may want or need to take cash out of your plan. This will give you the opportunity to make provisions for planned expenditures long before you ever need to come up with the money to pay for them. You could put aside money for your children's education, the trip to Australia you've always wanted to take, buying a sailboat, or building that vacation home on the lot you own in the desert. Building in perks for yourself is one of the most important parts of a successful plan and a great way to stay connected to your plan's ultimate success.

Sometimes you may have enough money in your property accounts to pay for the things you want. If that's the case, then you'll be able to keep the status quo on your buildings and still dip in for some of the things you want. Alternatively, significant cash withdrawals can occur in two ways:

1. By selling your property

2. By refinancing your property

**Other Goals.** This section covers other things you would like to accomplish with some of the earnings from your real estate investments. These could involve donations to charity or help to family and friends. Examples of these types of goals are:

- Buying a time-share condominium as a wedding present for the kids when they get married.

- Donating 10 percent of the expected proceeds from the sale of the Lawndale duplex to Notre Dame's scholarship fund.

- Purchasing a new theater curtain for the local playhouse.

## GENERAL PLAN

Your general plan will spell out in one sentence how you will achieve your goals over the period of time set forth. As we have already seen, setting future net worth at a given interest rate also sets future cash flow. Therefore, we will concentrate most of our discussion of the general plan on achieving a given future net worth.

Here is the template for your general plan:

"I am going to invest $ _____ for _____
years in real estate investments at a sustained rate of
return of _____ % and be worth $ _____
at the end of the plan term."

The first step in developing this general plan is figuring
out what you can reasonably expect to earn. We teased you
with what is possible earlier, and now we will show you
the real numbers in earnest. The chart in Figure 5.1 shows
various combinations of the compound interest formula.
It will quickly give you an idea of the kind of future equities
you might expect at various times with differing investment
amounts.

Going down the left column (Present Value), locate the
amount you originally plan to invest in real estate. Let's say
it's $10,000. Move over one column to the right to locate
the number of years you plan on being invested (n). For
this example, we'll say it will be twenty. The columns to the
right of that number are the future values (FV) based on
the interest you will be earning (I). Here we are being pretty
conservative and projecting an average return of 20 percent
for your real estate investments. This gives us a final value
at the end of twenty years of $383,376. These numbers don't
lie. Feel free to do the math and see for yourself how they add
up. What's more, go ahead and make copies of this chart and
post them above your bed because these are the numbers
that will help you quit your day job for good.

Figure 5.1

## PRESENT VALUE/FUTURE VALUE CHART

| Present Value | Number of Years | Interest = 10% | Interest = 20% | Interest = 30% | Interest = 40% |
|---|---|---|---|---|---|
| $10,000 | 5 | $ 16,105 | $ 24,883 | $ 37,129 | $ 53,782 |
| | 10 | $ 25,937 | $ 61,917 | $ 137,858 | $ 289,255 |
| | 15 | $ 41,772 | $ 154,070 | $ 511,859 | $ 1,555,681 |
| | 20 | $ 67,275 | $ 383,376 | $ 1,900,496 | $ 8,366,826 |
| $20,000 | 5 | $ 32,210 | $ 49,766 | $ 74,259 | $ 107,565 |
| | 10 | $ 51,875 | $ 123,835 | $ 275,717 | $ 578,509 |
| | 15 | $ 83,545 | $ 308,140 | $ 1,023,718 | $ 3,111,362 |
| | 20 | $134,550 | $ 766,752 | $ 3,800,993 | $16,733,651 |
| $30,000 | 5 | $ 48,315 | $ 74,650 | $ 111,388 | $ 161,347 |
| | 10 | $ 77,812 | $ 185,752 | $ 413,575 | $ 867,764 |
| | 15 | $125,317 | $ 462,211 | $ 1,535,577 | $ 4,667,043 |
| | 20 | $201,825 | $1,150,128 | $ 5,701,489 | $25,100,477 |
| $40,000 | 5 | $ 64,420 | $ 99,533 | $ 148,517 | $ 215,130 |
| | 10 | $103,750 | $ 247,669 | $ 551,434 | $ 1,157,019 |
| | 15 | $167,090 | $ 616,281 | $ 2,047,436 | $ 6,222,724 |
| | 20 | $269,100 | $1,533,504 | $ 7,601,986 | $33,467,302 |
| $50,000 | 5 | $ 80,526 | $ 124,416 | $ 185,647 | $ 268,912 |
| | 10 | $129,687 | $ 309,587 | $ 689,292 | $ 1,446,273 |
| | 15 | $208,862 | $ 770,351 | $ 2,559,295 | $ 7,778,405 |
| | 20 | $336,375 | $1,916,880 | $ 9,502,482 | $41,834,128 |
| $60,000 | 5 | $ 96,631 | $ 149,299 | $ 222,776 | $ 322,694 |
| | 10 | $155,625 | $ 371,504 | $ 827,151 | $ 1,735,528 |
| | 15 | $250,635 | $ 924,421 | $ 3,071,154 | $ 9,334,086 |
| | 20 | $403,650 | $2,300,256 | $11,402,978 | $50,200,953 |

Now that you can see how compound interest will be your best friend, let's pull all this work together and set your general plan. There are three steps in the process:

1. Determine how much cash you have available to invest comfortably.

2. Set the achievability of your future net worth.

3. Set the number of years you want for the overall plan.

We'll go through the same exercise as before, but this time it won't be a dress rehearsal. Using this chart, move down the column on the far left (Present Value) to the amount nearest your available capital. Move across this row until you come to a value at least as large as your lump-sum gap or your future net-worth goal. The percentage rate at the top of this column is the minimum rate of return you will have to maintain in order to meet your general plan goal in the time you have allotted to achieve it. Remember, you can combine two lines and add the totals to get a combination that equals your capital investment if it isn't on the chart.

## DETAILED PLAN

Figure 5.2 is similar to a business profit plan. It establishes the year-by-year goals and will be the yardstick by which to measure how you are doing along the way. Make copies of the worksheet in Figure 5.2 and insert them in your

FIGURE 5.2

## TRANSACTIONAL POSITION WORKSHEET

*Starting Year* _____

*Transactional Position for Real Estate Retirement Plan*

| Year of Plan | Market Value | Total Equity | Income | Oper'g Exp's | Total Interest | Amortization | Cash Flow | Appreciation | Tax Savings | Return on Equity % | Avg. Return on Equity % |
|---|---|---|---|---|---|---|---|---|---|---|---|
| | Actual | Actual | __% x Yearly Increase | __% x Yearly Increase | Actual | Actual | Actual | __% x Market Value | Actual | | |
| 1 | | | | | | | | | | | |
| 2 | | | | | | | | | | | |
| 3 | | | | | | | | | | | |
| 4 | | | | | | | | | | | |
| 5 | | | | | | | | | | | |
| 6 | | | | | | | | | | | |
| 7 | | | | | | | | | | | |
| 8 | | | | | | | | | | | |
| 9 | | | | | | | | | | | |
| 10 | | | | | | | | | | | |
| 11 | | | | | | | | | | | |
| 12 | | | | | | | | | | | |
| 13 | | | | | | | | | | | |
| 14 | | | | | | | | | | | |
| 15 | | | | | | | | | | | |
| 16 | | | | | | | | | | | |
| 17 | | | | | | | | | | | |
| 18 | | | | | | | | | | | |
| 19 | | | | | | | | | | | |
| 20 | | | | | | | | | | | |

planning binder. You should be adding data to it for as long as you're building your nest egg through real estate.

The rows represent the year by using year-by-year estimates of the performance of any property you acquire. The columns are the financial parameters of the plan.

The most important columns are the last two: Return on Equity and Average Return on Equity. The numbers that are inserted into these columns are the ones that need to stay above the minimum percentage return required to meet your goals in your desired time frame.

To illustrate how to do this and to make it really simple, we will use the $182,500 it took to buy the four-unit building in Long Beach, California, in chapter three as our starting capital. We'll use that property as the beginning investment of this example and the general investment plan that we just worked out to set our final net worth goal.

> "We are going to invest $182,500 for twenty years in real estate investments at a sustained rate of return of 20 percent to be worth $320,886 at the end of the plan term."

Given that goal, the next step in creating a detailed plan is to establish accurate variables to be used to make the estimates for the future calculations. What you will need are:

- appreciation rate for your area;
- interest rates for first and second loans;
- loan-to-value ratios;
- income and expense increase rates;
- buy and sell costs; and
- gross multipliers for various size properties.

You will be able to establish these variables after you have conducted some diligent research. Also, don't discount the help that the agent who sold you your property might be able to give. He or she should have access to the prior history of the market, appreciation rates, and all the other variables needed to help establish a detailed plan. We will start this detailed plan with the specifics of the example property at the end of the first year of ownership.

To recap (see Figure 5.3), remember that in our example our return on investment the first year was:

| | |
|---|---|
| Cash Flow | $     12 |
| Equity Growth (loan reduction) | $  2,664 |
| Equity Growth (appreciation) | $13,950 |
| Tax Benefits | $  1,106 |
| Total | $17,732 |

To make the estimates for the second and succeeding years of the plan, we have used the assumption of a 3.5 percent yearly income increase and a 2.5 percent yearly increase in expenses. For the other components on the chart, we have worked out the actual numbers in longhand. This requires a bit of time and arithmetic but is necessary for you to be accurate.

The next chart in Figure 5.4 takes us through the end of the third year of ownership on the Long Beach four-unit.

As they say, "The proof is in the pudding." By penciling out your year-by-year transactional position, the idea is you will be able to stay on track and retire on schedule.

FIGURE 5.3

## TRANSACTIONAL POSITION WORKSHEET- 2012

*Starting Year 2012*

*Transactional Position for Real Estate Retirement Plan*

| Year of Plan | Market Value | Total Equity | Income | Oper'g Exp's | Total Interest | Amorti-zation | Cash Flow | Appre-ciation | Tax Savings | Return on Equity % | Avg. Return on Equity % |
|---|---|---|---|---|---|---|---|---|---|---|---|
| | Actual | Actual | _% x Yearly Increase | _% x Yearly Increase | Actual | Actual | Actual | _% x Market Value | Actual | | |
| 1 | 279,000 | 8,370 | 27,000 | 5,400 | 18,948 | 2,664 | 12 | 13,950 | 1,106 | 212 | 212 |
| 2 | | | | | | | | | | | |
| 3 | | | | | | | | | | | |
| 4 | | | | | | | | | | | |
| 5 | | | | | | | | | | | |
| 6 | | | | | | | | | | | |
| 7 | | | | | | | | | | | |
| 8 | | | | | | | | | | | |
| 9 | | | | | | | | | | | |
| 10 | | | | | | | | | | | |
| 11 | | | | | | | | | | | |
| 12 | | | | | | | | | | | |
| 13 | | | | | | | | | | | |
| 14 | | | | | | | | | | | |
| 15 | | | | | | | | | | | |
| 16 | | | | | | | | | | | |
| 17 | | | | | | | | | | | |
| 18 | | | | | | | | | | | |
| 19 | | | | | | | | | | | |
| 20 | | | | | | | | | | | |

FIGURE 5.4

## TRANSACTIONAL POSITION WORKSHEET— THREE YEARS

*Starting Year 2012*

*Transactional Position for Real Estate Retirement Plan*

| Year of Plan | Market Value | Total Equity | Income | Oper'g Exp's | Total Interest | Amorti-zation | Cash Flow | Appre-ciation | Tax Savings | Return on Equity % | Avg. Return on Equity % |
|---|---|---|---|---|---|---|---|---|---|---|---|
| | Actual | Actual | __% x Yearly Increase | __% x Yearly Increase | Actual | Actual | Actual | __% x Market Value | Actual | | |
| 1 | 279,000 | 8,370 | 27,000 | 5,400 | 18,948 | 2,664 | 12 | 13,950 | 1,106 | 212 | 212 |
| 2 | 292,950 | 22,320 | 27,945 | 5,535 | 18,757 | 2,855 | 798 | 14,648 | 1,110 | 87 | 149 |
| 3 | 307,598 | 369,968 | 28,923 | 5,673 | 18,557 | 3,055 | 1,638 | 15,380 | 1,060 | 57 | 118 |
| 4 | | | | | | | | | | | |
| 5 | | | | | | | | | | | |
| 6 | | | | | | | | | | | |
| 7 | | | | | | | | | | | |
| 8 | | | | | | | | | | | |
| 9 | | | | | | | | | | | |
| 10 | | | | | | | | | | | |
| 11 | | | | | | | | | | | |
| 12 | | | | | | | | | | | |
| 13 | | | | | | | | | | | |
| 14 | | | | | | | | | | | |
| 15 | | | | | | | | | | | |
| 16 | | | | | | | | | | | |
| 17 | | | | | | | | | | | |
| 18 | | | | | | | | | | | |
| 19 | | | | | | | | | | | |
| 20 | | | | | | | | | | | |

## FOLLOW-UP AND GOAL REVIEW

This is the section of the planning binder that you will revisit on a regular basis. Here, you should insert predetermined dates to periodically monitor your progress. Certainly more important than assembling a successful plan on paper, will be managing it to its successful completion. This section of your plan will force you to review and adjust your thinking at each step along the way.

This review of your plan starts with objectively looking at your personal situation and then examining how changes in your life may affect your investments. You will see that you might need to adjust your long-term goals. For example, an unexpected promotion at work may allow you to buy another building sooner than expected. This could get you to your goal sooner or raise the amount of your final net worth when it comes time to retire. On the other hand, a job change may take away some of the time you had dedicated to the properties and could slow things down. Furthermore, the market and the economy may be changing for better or worse, which would, no doubt, affect what you buy and sell in the coming year.

We recommend you keep a blank copy of the transactional projection worksheet (Figure 5.2). When you do a follow-up and goal review, make it a point to meet with your investment real estate agent and get an estimate of value based on the current market conditions. Compare what really happened in that year with the plan you laid out one year earlier. See how you did. If there are any significant changes, go back and revise your plan and get ready for next year. Ask your agent's opinion on how the market is doing and where it looks like it is going in the next twelve months. Use the new value and the actual performance figures from the year's operation of your property to complete the next line of your transactional position worksheet.

No doubt, many changes will occur over the life of a long-term real estate investment plan. Some changes will be positive and some will be negative. The secret is to take full advantage of the positives and take the necessary steps to minimize the negatives. This requires keeping informed at all times about what's really happening with you and the market.

"After playing ten years in the National Hockey League, all my investments were in the stock or bond markets. After retiring, I started investing in apartment buildings by purchasing two four-unit buildings. Since then I have bought seven more buildings. Over the last ten years we have made over ten times more through apartments than the last twenty years in the stock market. Now our portfolio is built through our apartment complexes, thanks to Buckingham Investments [where Martin Stone was a broker]."

—Jamie S.

—— **CRITICAL CONCEPT** ——

## Invest in Real Estate—It Never Goes Out of Business

Any time you make an investment, you take on some risk. That risk can become greater for many reasons, and usually the higher the potential gain, the higher the risk. For most of us, the primary places we can invest are the stock market or real estate. What we feel is the greatest advantage of real estate is it never goes out of business. Admittedly, the real estate industry does go through cycles, but when those down cycles are over, the property is still there producing income for its owners. In reality, during those down cycles, the only owners who are affected are those who are forced to sell during tough times. In many areas of our country, there are properties that date back to the early 1900s and even into the late 1800s that are still in use today. In contrast, look at the history of the S&P 500, the American stock market index (*PR Newswire*, March 2, 2007). It claims to represent 75 percent of the largest companies in the United States. On its fiftieth anniversary, it announced that eighty-six of "the original constituents survived through time." That's 17.2 percent of the original companies! I'm sure there are plenty of areas where you are considering investing that are over fifty years old and still doing well, but going out of business when you own real estate is one major risk you don't have to worry about.

# PART 2

# Digging Deeper

# 6

# The IRS Is Your Best Partner

*"Late one night, just blocks from the Capitol, a mugger jumped into the path of a well-dressed fellow and stuck a gun in his ribs. 'Give me your money,' the thief demanded. 'Are you kidding?' the man said. 'I'm a US congressman.' 'In that case,' the mugger growled, cocking his weapon, 'give me my money.'"*

—*Playboy* Magazine

Owning investment real estate comes with a slew of tax ramifications. Thankfully, if tax rules are used to their full advantage, the IRS seems to line up clearly on the right side of the investor. Even so, lawmakers often manipulate tax codes to either stimulate or restrain the economy as they see fit. Whether it's making changes to the depreciation schedules or battling back and forth about capital gains laws, the one constant from the IRS is that nothing ever stays the same. Regardless, the tax benefits from owning investment real estate can be substantial. In this chapter, I'll explain how Uncle Sam is there to help you retire in style.

There are two broad areas where knowledge of taxation rules is important. The first is during the ownership and management of real estate. The second is on the sale of real estate. I hope both of these areas are ones that you will become intimately familiar with. I'll begin by talking about the tax laws related to ownership and management of real property.

## DEDUCTIONS AS AN OWNER

As a property owner, you are allowed, by the IRS, to deduct most of the purchase costs and operating expenses associated with a real estate purchase. The rule says that purchase costs are deductible in the year in which you acquire the property. The following list covers some of the most common items that are deductible:

- Prepaid interest on your loans

- Fire insurance

- Liability insurance

- Property tax prorations

- Escrow fees

- Title insurance costs

- Miscellaneous fees from lender

- Miscellaneous fees from escrow company

In addition, loan fees and points paid to secure a new loan on income property are deductible. The difference is these fees must be paid off over the life of the loan as opposed to in the year of acquisition. For instance, if the four-unit property in Long Beach, California, in chapters three and five required a loan fee of 1.5 percent and the loan was for thirty years, the yearly deduction would first be calculated by multiplying the loan amount by the loan fee rate:

| | |
|---|---|
| Loan Amount | $143,600 |
| Loan Fee Rate | × .015 |
| Loan Fee (points) | $  2,154 |

Then, to determine your yearly deduction, divide the loan fee by the term of the loan:

Loan Fee ($2,154) ÷ Term of Loan (30 years) = $71.80

## OPERATING EXPENSES

Operating expenses for your rental property are deductible in the year you spend the money. The problem is distinguishing between items to be expensed and items to be capitalized. As mentioned, the IRS says that expense items are deductible in the year you spend the money. Capital expenses, however, are a different story. These items must be written off over the period of time they contribute to their useful life under the tax codes.

For those just starting out in this game, distinguishing between capital items and items to be expensed can be tricky. As a general rule, if any improvement you make increases the value or completely replaces a component of the property, it should be considered a capital expenditure and needs to be depreciated over time. In contrast, if the improvement merely maintains the value or corrects a problem at your building, then it should be considered an expense item. Some examples of items you can expense yearly are:

- Utility payments

- Interest on loans

- Taxes

- Insurance premiums

- Gardening and cleaning costs

- Business licenses and city fees

- Plumbing repairs

- Roofing repairs

- Electrical repairs

- Miscellaneous maintenance and repairs

- Property management fees

- Advertising and rental commissions

- Mileage, postage, and phone expenses associated with the operation of the property

- Any other noncapital expenses

As you can see, these items maintain the value and/or correct problems. Thus, you are able to expense them.

## CAPITAL EXPENSES

A capital expense is money spent on major improvements to rental property, such as building additions and all permanent fixtures on a property. Some examples of capital expenses are:

- Drapes or window coverings
- Carpeting
- New roof
- New plumbing
- New electrical system
- Building additions
- Major appliances or furnishings
- Major repairs (new driveway, replace siding or stucco, replace landscaping, etc.)

It is important to note that unlike interest (an item you can expense yearly), the money that goes toward principal each month on your loan payment is not a deductible capital expense. It is actually one of those returns on your investment that you must pay tax on but don't get the money for. The reason that the part of the payment that goes toward principal reduction is taxable is because it's a profit that comes from tenant income.

## THE DEPRECIATION ALLOWANCE

We briefly covered some of the depreciation rules in chapter four, but because these rules are so vital to your bottom-line return, we'll dig a bit deeper.

As the owner of residential income property, you are now able to make a deduction for the loss of value to the building that sits on your property. This deduction is designed to compensate you for the wear and tear that happens to the physical structure from aging. This is not an allowance to cover you for the aging of the land because land does not wear out or depreciate.

The most important component of the depreciation schedule is the land-to-improvement ratio. For any improved property, part of a property's value comes from the dirt and part of its value comes from the improvements. Because dirt doesn't depreciate, a property that has a high ratio of improvements has a high depreciation deduction.

When determining depreciation, you must remember that you can't just pick a ratio out of thin air. Instead, you must use a method accepted by the IRS. If you don't, the result could be costly. In a worst-case scenario, the IRS could audit you, disallow your schedule, and require you to set a new one. Odds are the IRS would end up charging you for additional taxes, penalties, and interest.

The safest method in setting your land-to-improvement ratio is to use the one that the county tax assessor sets on your tax bill. The good news is the IRS will rarely challenge this ratio, as it would be challenging another government entity. Unfortunately, the ratio determined by the county tax assessor isn't always as accurate as it could be. Alternatively, you could derive a ratio from the appraisal that was conducted when you purchased your property. Using an appraisal is a good idea, especially if the tax assessor's ratio doesn't agree with the actual market.

Once you have established an accurate value of the improvements, the calculation to determine your depreciation deduction is fairly easy.

As a final point, you must remember that the depreciation schedule you originally calculate will be with you as long as you own that property. If you sell the property and pay the taxes due, you can start fresh with a new depreciation schedule on your next building. If you trade up via a 1031 exchange, however, that basis and its schedule stay with you.

## CAPITAL GAINS

Capital gains taxes are taxes on the profits you make when you sell your property. To help determine capital gains, you must first learn some new tax terms:

- Sale price: the price you sell your property for

- Adjusted sale price: the net price after subtracting costs of the sale

- Cost basis: the original purchase price plus capital expenses

- Adjusted cost basis: the cost basis less depreciation

Now that you're up to speed on the terminology, you can see that capital gains can be estimated by first subtracting the sale costs from the sale price. This computation gives you the adjusted sale price:

Sale Price
− Sale Costs
Adjusted Sale Price

To determine the adjusted cost basis, take the original purchase price, add in capital expenses, and then subtract depreciation:

> Original Purchase Price
> + Capital Expenses
> − Depreciation
> _____
> Adjusted Cost Basis

Finally, to determine your capital gain, subtract the adjusted cost basis from the adjusted sale price:

> Adjusted Sale Price
> − Adjusted Cost Basis
> _____
> Capital Gain

Now let's use an illustration with our example four-unit Long Beach property to calculate the capital gain. Remember, we bought the property for $179,500. We've depreciated it for twenty-five years at $4,890 per year, which is a total depreciation of $122,250. Twenty-five years later, we can sell the property for $729,500. Our total expense to sell will be $51,000. Knowing all this, we can calculate our capital gain on a sale by going through the simple calculations you just learned:

| | |
|---|---:|
| Sale Price | $729,500 |
| Less Sale Costs | − 51,000 |
| Adjusted Sale Price | $678,500 |
| | |
| Cost Basis | $179,500 |
| Less Depreciation | − 122,250 |
| Adjusted Cost Basis | $57,250 |

| Adjusted Sale Price | $678,500 |
|---|---|
| Adjusted Cost Basis | −57,250 |
| Capital Gain | $621,250 |

As you see, the capital gain in this scenario would be $621,250. Thankfully, a number of options are available to the real estate investor to help defer paying these taxes. What follows are the methods that help distinguish real estate investing from all other investment vehicles.

## THE 1031 TAX-DEFERRED EXCHANGE

When it comes to deferring capital gains taxes, the IRS 1031 tax-deferred exchange is probably the real estate investor's single most important technique available. By using the 1031 exchange, you can pyramid your equity and continue to defer your taxes for years into the future. In effect, the IRS becomes your business partner by letting you use the taxes you owe on your capital gain as a down payment on the building you trade into. The government figures that when you trade into larger properties, you will, in turn, make more profit. By making more profit, you will eventually owe more taxes. As far as the IRS is concerned, everyone wins. Who said Uncle Sam can't be your friend?

Three rules must be adhered to when qualifying for a 1031 exchange:

1. You must trade for like-kind property. In this instance, like-kind would mean the property you are trading into would be for investment purposes. For example, you can't trade an income-producing

duplex for a getaway beach cottage. In contrast, you could trade that duplex for a strip mall or another apartment building. The idea is to trade income-producing property for other income-producing property.

2. The new property should be of equal or greater value than the existing property. This means that you can't trade a four-unit that you sold for $729,500 for a triplex worth $500,000. Rather, the new property needs to be worth more than the old one. Hence the phrase "trading up."

3. You should not receive cash, mortgage relief, or boot (boot is defined by the IRS as taxable proceeds from a sale other than cash) of any kind in the transaction.

## TYPES OF 1031 EXCHANGES

Most 1031 tax-deferred exchanges fall into one of three categories:

1. Straight Exchange

2. Three-party Exchange

3. Delayed Exchange

The straight exchange happens when two parties simply trade properties. At the end of the transaction, each party goes his or her own way. In truth, this scenario doesn't occur that often. Most property owners either trade up or get out altogether. By trading straight across the board, one party probably ends up with a lesser property, which fails to meet the requirements of trading into a property of equal or greater value. If this were the case, the party that got the lesser property would have to pay the taxes due, if any.

The most common exchange is the three-party exchange. As its name suggests, three different parties are involved in the process. One of the key elements of a 1031 exchange is that the party trading up never receives the equity in the property being traded. For that reason, the party cannot just sell the property, collect the proceeds, and go out and buy a larger property. Because most people with bigger properties don't want to trade into anything smaller (and thereby have to pay any taxes owed), these three-party exchanges have evolved so that each party can get what it wants and stay within the framework of the law. Here's how a three-party exchange might work:

Facts:

- Andrew owns a triplex and wants to trade into a six-unit building.

- Barry owns a six-unit building and wants to sell, pay his capital gains taxes, and retire along the Gulf of Mexico.

- Charlie is just getting started investing and wants to buy the triplex that Andrew owns.

Solution:

Andrew and Barry enter into an exchange escrow in which Andrew gets the six-unit and Barry gets title to the triplex. In a separate escrow, Barry agrees to accommodate the exchange and deed the triplex to Charlie immediately after he acquires title from Andrew. Both of these escrows contain contingencies stating that they must close concurrently. This means that if Charlie can't buy the triplex for some reason, Barry will not have to take Andrew's triplex in trade for his six-unit building.

Result:

At the close, Charlie got started investing and now owns the triplex he wanted; Andrew traded up into the six-unit building he desired; and Barry is relaxing in retirement, sipping drinks with little umbrellas in them along the Gulf of Mexico.

In case you were wondering, Barry doesn't pay any tax by taking the title to the triplex because it is sold for the same price at which it was taken in trade. This is what is called a "nontaxable event."

The last type of exchange is the delayed or "Starker" exchange. Starker refers to one of the principals in *T. J. Starker v. United States*, a case from the US Court of Appeals for the Ninth Circuit. In this case, Starker swapped some timber acreage for eleven different parcels of property owned by Crown Zellerbach Corporation. As agreed between the parties, Starker chose the properties, and they were conveyed to him by way of the exchange. It was deemed a delayed exchange because the process spanned more than two years.

Because of the two-year delay, Uncle Sam questioned whether it was an exchange at all and took Starker to court. Fortunately for all of us, the court of appeals approved of the process, which has since been codified nationally for use by all real estate investors. The court held that:

1. A simultaneous transfer of title was not required; and

2. Internal Revenue Code (IRC) section 1031 should be broadly interpreted and applied. Treasury regulations under IRC section 1001 to the contrary were held invalid.

Once the court made its rulings, a number of additional changes were made to IRC 1031. These changes included:

1. The exchange property the taxpayer desires to receive must be identified within forty-five days after the date on which the taxpayer transfers his or her property in the exchange.

2. The taxpayer must receive the identified property within the earlier of 180 days after the date he or she transfers his or her property in the exchange, or the due date of his or her tax return for the year of the exchange, including extensions.

As with all tax issues, make sure you consult with your own tax professional before making any decisions in this regard.

To accomplish a delayed exchange, an accommodator is used. An accommodator is an unrelated party or entity that holds the exchange proceeds and then purchases the trade properties to complete the exchange. In choosing an accommodator, you need to exercise due care. Remember that all the funds from your sale will be in its hands until you close on your property. To that end, make sure you check out your accommodator's credentials through the Better Business Bureau and your state real estate department.

One final issue that exchanges create is related to the goals from your investment plan. While the use of the exchange allows you to "pyramid" equities, it also pyramids the tax liability on a future sale. If you had plans of cashing out and paying your taxes before retiring, this could leave you with a big tax bill. Instead, you might consider one of two other options. Either pay your taxes as you go along or consider the next alternative, the installment sale.

## THE INSTALLMENT SALE

The installment sale is another significant technique for deferring payment of capital gains taxes. Here, sellers elect not only to sell property but also to put up some or all of the financing needed to make the deal work. Because the property is being sold now but paid for later, such deals are called "installment sales." Where taxes are concerned, an installment sale differs from the 1031 exchange because you actually sell the property without getting a new one in return, but you still defer paying some or most of your capital gains taxes. Here's how:

> Until you actually receive the profit from the sale of your property, you don't owe the IRS a penny. Instead, with an installment sale, you would be carrying the note (and your profit from the sale) long-term and receiving interest-only payments from the buyer. The idea is to keep earning a high interest on the taxes due for many years. By doing this, you would delay paying the capital gains until the contract is complete.

The rules for qualifying for an installment sale were significantly modified by the Installment Sales Revision Act of 1980. In the past, there were rules regarding the amount of down payment and the number of years needed to qualify. These no longer exist. Now, the advantage of an installment sale is you are required to pay capital gains tax only on the amount of the profit you receive in one year. You pay the balance of the tax due as you collect the profit in subsequent years.

Because an installment sale can be relatively complex, I advise you to get a certified public accountant to review any installment sale you might be considering. There may be tax due on the recapture of prior years' depreciation in addition to the capital gains tax.

As mentioned, with an installment sale, instead of selling the property, getting all cash, and walking, you become the lender on the property.

Let's assume you sell the four-unit Long Beach property for $729,500 and are willing to take a 20 percent down payment and carry the balance on an installment contract. Here is how this scenario would look:

| | |
|---|---|
| Sale Price | $729,500 |
| Less Down Payment | −145,900 |
| Installment Loan | $583,600 |

In this example, you end up with an installment note on the property of $583,600.

In the following illustrations, you will see how the real advantage of an installment sale comes from what you earn from the installment note, as opposed to putting your net cash in the bank. Today you can get 1.5 percent interest on your savings from a CD or a similar investment. Because you often can earn greater yields by carrying the note, we'll assume that you can hold this financing at 6 percent interest.

For starters, let's illustrate what the profit on a CD or a similar investment would look like:

| | |
|---|---|
| Profit | $583,600 |
| Interest Rate | x   .015 |
| Profit | $  8,754 |
| Monthly Return | $     730 |

Here is the return on an installment note:

| Installment Note | $583,600 |
|---|---|
| Interest Rate | x    .06 |
| Profit | $  35,016 |
| Monthly Return | $   2,918 |

If you divide the total installment profit by twelve months, you create an income for yourself of $2,918 per month.

Varying the amount of down payment you accept can increase this interest profit even more. In theory, because you are the banker on your loan, you could agree to a zero down deal and only require interest-only payments. By doing so, you would not have to pay any tax whatsoever at this time. Instead, you could be earning 6 percent on your entire note.

## REFINANCING

There is one more technique to avoid paying the taxes due on some of the profit from your real estate. This is by securing new financing to pay off the existing loan and net additional cash at the closing because of the increased value of the property. If you are still in the equity-building years of our plan, you will probably use that money to acquire an additional property. One of the great advantages of getting at some of the profit using this method is that there is no tax due on the money. Because we "borrowed" the money from the bank, we have to pay it back. Therefore, not only do we *not* have to pay any tax, but we also can write off the interest as a deduction on the property.

Owners who have properties that are managed particularly well prefer this technique. What's more, if you've correctly managed your property, the increased rents should more than cover any increased mortgage payments. If you are in a market where you can pull out most of your equity to move into another property and still keep the original property, you could be well on your way to creating a comfortable retirement scenario for yourself.

To sum up, this information is designed to give you a basic understanding of real estate taxation and some tax-deferral methods. The goal is to make you aware of the complexity of this area, so you will seek the advice of a tax expert before you make any move. When it comes to taxes, even minor mistakes could be costly. To that end, I recommend the following:

First, before you ever list a property for sale, make sure you schedule a general review meeting with a tax consultant. Review your goals, discuss all the alternatives, and get a general idea of your position.

Second, when listing a property for sale, make clear to your agent and in the listing contract that any transaction must be reviewed and approved by a tax consultant.

Finally, when negotiating a potential sale or exchange, include a contingency that gives you a right to have the final purchase agreement reviewed and approved by a tax consultant. This will give you an out if the tax expert advises you against the transaction.

—— $ ——

"I have spent my adult life accumulating property. I spent a great deal of time reading about markets and decided the United States offered great returns with a good legal system, and I then set about finding someone who could help. The last day of my last research trip, I came across Martin Stone at Buckingham Investments. Not only did everyone in the office get property, but within a short eight weeks I had purchased two four-unit buildings. They were to be the cornerstone of what is now a reasonably large portfolio of property I have in Los Angeles."

—*Jeremy L.*

# —— CRITICAL CONCEPT ——

## The Tax-Deferred Exchange

In this chapter, I say the IRS is your best partner for a good reason. Real estate is one of the few investments available to the average person where you can defer the tax you owe on the profit you make by doing an exchange for another larger investment. In theory, the tax will have to be paid someday, but using the money you owe the IRS to buy more property is a tremendous help in growing your wealth. Here's a quick example. Let's say you bought a property five years ago and have made a $300,000 long-term capital gain. The rates today can vary depending upon your tax bracket, but to show the benefit I will assume you are in the 20 percent bracket for capital gains tax. So for your $300,000 gain, you would have to pay $60,000 in tax. This would be $60,000 less you have to use as a down payment on your next property. Most investment property now takes 25 percent down payment, so this additional $60,000 will allow you to buy a property costing $240,000 ($60,000 ÷ .25 = $240,000).

# 7

# Appraising Value

*"A pint of sweat saves a gallon of blood."*

—General George S. Patton Jr.

For those just getting their feet wet in real estate investing, picking that first property can be a knee-knocking experience. Of course, the objective is to make your choice based on purely economic parameters. But, clearly, when it comes to taking a risk with your own hard-earned money, that can be easier said than done. Many times, when it comes to deciding between Property A and Property B, emotions will take over and attempt to dictate what you should buy. Many novice investors indignantly declare, "I refuse to purchase any building that I wouldn't live in." If you recognize yourself making that statement, you should realize that you're on the verge of leaving lots of great opportunities behind for someone else to discover.

But don't fret. You are not alone. In fact, it's easy to see why emotions rule the day. You're fearful of losing what little money you have been able to save. In fact, many will argue that the fear of losing their nest egg is as much, if not more of, a motivator as is the promise of gain from investing it. To illustrate, let's say you were invited to a get-together at 9:00 p.m. to learn about a business opportunity that could very well make you $1,000 on a $5,000 investment. After a bit of thought, you might decide to spend that time watching the news or sitcom reruns on TV instead. But let's turn the tables. What would happen if you got a call and were told you would lose that $1,000 if you didn't go to the 9:00 p.m. meeting? Precisely.

There is no shame in a bit of apprehension. In fact, playing the devil's advocate will usually help you make prudent decisions along the way. But beware! Unfounded fear about losing money by buying the "wrong" building could very well keep you from obtaining the perfect fit for your long-term plan. Thankfully, unlike investing in commodities such as stocks and bonds via the advice of a so-called expert, there are concrete things you can do that will minimize the risk of ever overpaying for a building—namely, learning how to value property accurately for yourself. Expert help is nice, but when it comes to protecting your own nest egg, the peace of mind that will come from conducting your own analysis will be nothing short of invaluable.

This chapter continues your education with a lesson on appraising value. I will teach you the same three classic methods of valuing property used by professional real estate appraisers. From here on, you should be able to buy real estate without the fear of ever losing your shirt.

## METHODS OF VALUING PROPERTY

Establishing the value of a piece of real estate can be a tricky job. Fortunately, there are a number of accepted methods of establishing value estimates. I will review each of these appraisal techniques and show you how to use them. The three commonly accepted appraisal methods used by professional appraisers are:

1.  Comparative Market Analysis

2.  Reproduction Cost

3.  Capitalization of Income

## COMPARATIVE MARKET ANALYSIS

"Comparative market analysis" means nothing more than doing some comparison shopping before you buy any real estate. Just as you would compare and shop prices before buying new furniture or a car, so, too, you need to compare and shop prices for similarly situated properties before making a purchase. The difference in this instance is that you are comparing a building that is for sale with ones that have already been sold.

What do you need to compare? The major considerations are:

•   Number of units

•   Square footage of the improvements (structure)

•   Square footage of the lot (the dirt)

- Condition of the surrounding neighborhood

- Age and condition of the building

- Income-producing capability (current rents versus market rents)

- Parking (garages, pads, carports, or none)

- Amenities (view, fireplaces, multiple baths, pool, patios or decks, etc.)

The idea when conducting a comparative market analysis is to locate a few properties that have recently been sold in the same or similar neighborhood. As outlined previously, look for properties that have traits similar to the one you want to buy. In a perfect world, the sales should be within the past six months. The more recent, the better. Once you gather all the data, your job is to compare and contrast it to determine a fair price for the building you're considering.

## REPRODUCTION COST

Another way to estimate the actual value of a property is to use what is known as the "reproduction cost" method. That is, what would it cost to build that same building today? Here you pretend to buy a lot at today's value and then build a "used" building that matches the existing building. For this reason alone, this is not an easy method. It requires a good knowledge of the market for raw land as well as an understanding of the costs of construction and depreciation. Consequently, this method is often used solely by professional real estate appraisers.

## CAPITALIZATION OF INCOME

The last method of appraising real estate value is called the "capitalization of income." This approach determines a building's value based on its profitability. In the real world of appraising, different processes of valuing property are used for different types of buildings. With single-family homes, the comparative market analysis method is used most often. The reproduction cost method is usually employed for specialized properties (like a church) and for new construction. But for investment property of multiple units, the capitalization of income method is best.

This is probably the most difficult of the three methods to use properly when valuing income property, but it is the preferred method. For starters, it might help to think of capitalization rates as interest rates. When you put money in the bank, you ask, "What interest rate will I get?" Capitalization rates are the same thing. Let's assume you have $10,000 in a savings account and at the end of the year you earned $500 in interest. The following formula will show your interest rate:

Interest Earned ÷ Amount Invested = Interest Rate

Or plugging the savings account numbers into the equation, we get:

$$\$500 \div \$10,000 = 5\%$$

Similarly, to determine the capitalization rate on a building, divide the net income by its price. Net income is determined by subtracting the operating expenses from the gross income. The equation looks like this:

Gross Income – Operating Expenses ÷ Price
= Capitalization Rate

Or

Net Income ÷ Price = Capitalization Rate

Using this formula, you can calculate the capitalization rate (or interest rate) you will earn on any investment you are considering. Once you know the capitalization rate of your proposed property, you then can determine its value. To do so, you need to change the formulas as follows:

Gross Income – Operating Expenses ÷ Capitalization Rate
= Price

Simplified, this becomes:

Net Income ÷ Capitalization Rate = Price

Because this valuation method is so useful, it behooves you to really understand how to use it. To do so accurately, you need to know a few things about the proposed property, including:

- gross income;
- operating expenses; and
- capitalization rate investors expect in the area where the property is located.

Let's review the capitalization rate.

## THE CAPITALIZATION RATE

The final item needed for this valuation method is the expected capitalization rate. The capitalization rate is determined by understanding how much of a return investors can expect to realize in a particular market. The rate will vary in different parts of the country, in different parts of a city, even in buildings within a few blocks of each other.

Additionally, residential, commercial, and industrial properties have varying capitalization rates. Remember, because the capitalization rate measures the profitability of an investment, certain types of properties involve other risks and thus dissimilar profit possibilities.

## GROSS RENT MULTIPLIER

Sometimes you need a quick way to analyze the value of a building that can get you to the bottom line fast. When this is the case, it is good to know about a method called "the gross rent multiplier." Similar to a price-earnings ratio when valuing a stock, the gross rent multiplier presupposes there is a number—the gross rent multiplier—that you can multiply by the gross income of a property to quickly estimate its value.

Here's how you determine that magic number, the gross rent multiplier:

Price of Property ÷ Gross Income = Gross Rent Multiplier

So the lesson to remember is that the gross rent multiplier is only a rule of thumb. It is not nearly as accurate as the other three methods of appraisal (comparative market analysis, reproduction cost, capitalization of income), but it does provide a quick way to rank properties when you are initially looking around.

## HIGHEST AND BEST USE

Finally, one last concept you need to understand when analyzing and appraising investment property is called "highest and best use." Think about a time when you drove through a commercial area, only to see an old farm or single-family home that looked completely out of place. If you wanted to buy that property, the question is "Should it be appraised as a residence or as a commercial lot?" The answer is probably a commercial lot because that would be the property's highest and best use.

Awareness of a building's highest and best use can yield hidden profits. Each of the following properties, for example, would warrant a valuation as its highest and best use rather than its current use:

- A house in an industrial area

- Small units on a large lot zoned for multiunits in an area with many new buildings

- Buildings that may sit on two separate lots

- An apartment house with large one-bedroom apartments that could be made into two bedrooms simply by adding a wall and a door

- A small house on a multiunit-zoned plot where extra units can be added

- A vacant commercial building that can be converted to loft apartments

Properties like these can and should be valued in more than one way. The highest and best use for the property may not be its current use. Note, however, that the highest and best use is not always obvious, as in the case of the building that sits on two lots.

The moral of the story is that real estate investing is a multidimensional task. Failure to look at all aspects may mean failure to realize the full potential of your investment. It is important to discover any hidden profits that lie waiting to be tapped.

—— $ ——

"I found out about Buckingham Investments by doing loans for clients of the company while I was working for a major saving and loan in the LA area. From my customers I learned about all the education they provided for their clients and the research and planning that they did. I started working with them for that reason about twenty years ago. I have bought close to 200 units over the years which has allowed me to retire while most of the people I worked with are still in the lending business."

—Jim S.

# —— CRITICAL CONCEPT ——

## History Teacher or Fortune Teller

An important step in buying a property is doing an appraisal of value based upon historical sales information. This is almost always required by the lender who will make your loan. This appraisal will be based upon data from prior sales and *will not* take into account current or future facts or potentials you see in the property as a long-term investor. These facts, coupled with your personal goals, in most cases, far outweigh this historical report that we call "an appraisal." Don't let this estimate of value from historical data deter you when you find a property with untapped potential that is a perfect fit for your investment goals.

# 8

# Financing Real Estate

*"If you would like to know the value of money, go and try
to borrow some."*

—Benjamin Franklin

L ocating the right financing is a critical piece to the real
estate investor's puzzle. Because many of us do not have
the money to buy property for all cash, we must borrow the
major portion of the purchase price from a lender.

In our four-unit Long Beach property, we used an FHA
loan, which required only 3 percent of the purchase price as
a down payment. This illustrates how even a nominal initial
investment could parlay itself into a serious nest egg over
time. When it comes time to buy, however, you may or may
not choose to finance your property this way. Therefore,
in this chapter I'll teach you how all real estate is financed,
break down the three major sources of money, and give you

tips on how to find the loan that will help bring you toward the promised land of financial independence.

## COSTS OF BORROWING

Let's first examine the costs connected with borrowing. As you start researching loan programs, you will find that the fees associated with borrowing could vary widely. Government lending programs will charge for one thing, while conventional lenders and private parties might charge for another. Two of the greatest factors affecting your costs will be who makes the loan and what type of loan it is. The list in Figure 8.1 covers the most common fees different lending institutions may charge.

Thankfully, the federal government has taken the guesswork out of determining which fees apply when borrowing money for real estate. The governing law is the Real Estate Settlement Procedures Act. RESPA requires that all lenders, except private parties, give borrowers an estimate of all the fees associated with their loans. Along with the RESPA estimate, the lender also must disclose the annual percentage rate of the loan. The APR will take into account all the fees that are paid on the loan up front to give a true picture of the annual interest rate that will be paid over the life of the loan.

The biggest expense is the loan fee or "points." Each point represents 1 percent of the loan amount. Points are expressed in terms of a percentage of the loan amount. For instance, if a loan costs a point and a half, this means that

Figure 8.1

**COMMON LENDING FEES**

|  | Government Loans | Conventional Loans | Private Loans |
|---|---|---|---|
| Loan Fee (Points) | X | X | |
| Appraisal Fee | X | X | |
| Credit Report | X | X | X |
| Tax Service | X | X | |
| Document Recording | X | X | |
| Loan Processing | X | X | |
| Drawing Documents | X | X | |
| Funding Fee | X | | |
| Prepaid Interest | X | X | |
| Mortgage Insurance | X | X | |
| Loan Escrow | X | X | X |
| Alta Title Insurance | X | X | |
| Setup | X | X | |
| Warehouse Fee | X | X | |

the cost will be 1.5 percent of the loan amount. For instance, 1.5 points on a $200,000 loan would be $3,000 in fees (1.5 × $200,000 = $3,000).

This cash expense is a sore point for most investors, yet it's an integral part of the lending business and one that you will end up having. This is because, for most loans, there is a normal point charge for the lender's standard rate loan. Many lenders advertise that they will make a zero-point loan.

It's important to note, however, that in doing so, they make up the points that they do not charge up front by charging more interest over the life of the loan.

The best way to decide which loan program is right for you is to do an analysis of each option. Compare the cost of the zero-point, higher interest rate loan to a loan where you pay a point or two at the onset. In most cases, you will probably find that it is better to pay for the points up front rather than pay for them over the life of your loan.

## THREE SOURCES OF MONEY

There are three primary sources to tap into when looking for a loan on residential real estate (one to four units). They are:

1. the federal government;
2. local savings and loans and banks; and
3. private parties.

For the remainder of this chapter, we will examine each of these sources in detail. Let's begin by seeing how Uncle Sam is willing to help.

## GOVERNMENT LENDING

As demonstrated earlier, the best source for government-supported financing for owner-occupied units is the Federal Housing Administration (FHA). Note that the FHA doesn't provide the actual funds for mortgages, but rather it insures home mortgage loans made by private industry lenders such as mortgage bankers, savings and loans, and banks.

This insurance is necessary because FHA loans are made with low down payment options and interest rates and terms compared with those of the conventional lending market.

The following chart illustrates the maximum FHA loan amounts available in high cost areas of California as of 2017. These limits change depending on which region of the country you're buying in, so make sure to check with a local lender to determine the limits in your area.

| Number of Units | High Cost |
| --- | --- |
| 1 | $ 636,150 |
| 2 | $ 814,500 |
| 3 | $ 984,525 |
| 4 | $1,223,475 |

One huge advantage of FHA loans is they offer great leverage to the investor. With a minimum requirement of just 3.5 percent down, these loans can be for as much as 96.5 percent of the purchase price. Remember, however, FHA's primary objective is to encourage home ownership for first-time buyers. Therefore, one stringent requirement of the FHA program is a buyer must live in the property for a period of time as his or her *primary* residence. For young people, this often works out great, but for those who already are established in their own homes, this requirement may put this loan out of reach.

It's no secret that the American dream is to own your own home. But if you can be patient, make your first purchase a set of FHA multiunits. The two- to four-unit market usually has the widest selection of properties available. By taking advantage of the value appreciation, in a few years you probably can refinance and move up to a single-family residence. At that time you will have a house to live in as well as a nice piece of income-producing property to boot!

Besides the great leverage you can attain via an FHA loan, another advantage to buying this way is these lenders are required to use FHA-approved appraisers. In addition to verifying the value of the building, the appraiser must make sure there are no major problems with the construction and that all the basic safety measures have been met. Luckily for buyers, the guidelines for upkeep are somewhat strict. In an instance where a structure doesn't hold up to FHA standards, the seller must either comply with the appraiser's requests to fix the problems or lose the deal. Once a real estate deal has been inked, however, sellers are rarely eager to let their deal slip away. In fact, smart real estate agents will do whatever it takes to make sure their sellers comply with FHA guidelines. More often than not, sellers do comply, and by the time of closing any deferred maintenance called out by the FHA appraiser will have been repaired.

## VA LOANS AND FIRST-TIME BUYER PROGRAMS

For veterans, Uncle Sam has provided a fantastic opportunity to buy an initial set of rental units. The government's help began just after World War II. The first veterans lending program was called the "GI Bill of Rights" and was intended to provide veterans with medical benefits, bonuses, and low-interest loans. VA loans are not directly made by the Department of Veterans Affairs but rather are guaranteed by it, which is similar to how FHA loans work. The wonderful thing about GI or veterans' loans is they can be obtained for 100 percent of the purchase price.

Finally, be sure to check out local resources; many communities offer first-time home buyer loans intended to help people purchase their first houses. Like FHA or VA loans, these first-time home buyer mortgages usually require the property to be owner-occupied and have low down payment options. City hall should be able to tell you if it has any such programs. If you qualify, these kinds of financing could give you a great head start toward preparing for retirement with little money out-of-pocket.

## CONVENTIONAL LOANS

Most people finance their real estate purchases through banks, savings and loans, or mortgage companies, and most of those loans are packaged using either the Federal National Mortgage Association (FNMA or Fannie Mae) or the Federal Home Loan Mortgage Corporation (Freddie Mac.) No matter what type of loan you choose, all conventional ones fall into one of two categories:

1. **Residential loans** are for properties that consist of a single-family home, a duplex, a triplex, or a fourplex.

2. **Commercial loans** are properties consisting of five units or more.

There are major differences between these two types of loans, including the number of lenders available, qualifications, and terms. Let's closely look at each loan.

## RESIDENTIAL LOANS: ONE TO FOUR UNITS

Residential loans come in unlimited forms. Here is an approximation of what you can expect: a standard conventional loan for these smaller units is for 75 percent of the appraised value of the property. Therefore, you will have to put down 25 percent.

You may hear about loans that offer 90, 95, or even 100 percent financing. These loans, indeed, existed in the past and may very well return as the real estate market stabilizes. Additionally, any loan less than 20 percent down will most likely require private mortgage insurance (PMI). PMI can be costly, but on the other hand paying for PMI allows you to buy real estate with less than 20 percent down, so it may be worth checking out.

Needless to say, residential loans are based on your creditworthiness and ability to repay the loan. This is calculated in two ways. First, lenders will look at your FICO score, which is based on a standardized credit rating system. According to the lender, the higher your FICO score, the lower of a risk you are. The other method of measuring your creditworthiness is by analyzing your debt-to-income ratio, which measures how much money you make versus how much you owe. After examining both of these numbers, most lenders will end up giving you an overall creditworthiness grade of A, B, C, or D. Here is a breakdown of their criteria:

- "A" credit. Very few or no credit problems within the past two years, one or two thirty-day late payments, a few small collections okay, and no more than one thirty-day late payment on your mortgage.

- "B" credit. A few late payments within the past eighteen months, up to four thirty-day late payments or up to two sixty-day late payments on revolving and installment debt, and one ninety-day late payment.

- "C" credit. Many thirty- to sixty-day late payments in the past two years, as well as late mortgage payments in the sixty- to ninety-day range. Bankruptcies and foreclosures that have been discharged or settled in the past twelve months are also part of this credit rating.

- "D" credit. Open collections, charge-offs, notice of defaults, etc., and several missed payments, bankruptcies, and/or foreclosures.

Of course, the lender will appraise the property in question as well, a decision that will most certainly figure into its decision to lend or not. This overall appraisal of you, your credit history, your job security, and to a lesser extent the property in question is what is important when applying for a loan on one to four units.

## COMMERCIAL LOANS: FIVE UNITS AND UP

When the loan you want is for five units and up, you will need to apply for a commercial loan. Unlike residential loan lenders, the commercial loan lender primarily will consider whether the property itself can generate a profit and not depend on your personal credit history and qualifying power. Another difference between commercial loans and residential loans is commercial loans are typically "nonrecourse" loans. Lenders cannot come after you personally if you default; they have no recourse.

Before making a loan on five units or more, lenders will want to see that the property will generate positive cash flow. This is called "debt coverage." The debt coverage they will want is normally 1.1 to 1.25 of the monthly debt payments. This means the property must have a net cash flow, after expenses and vacancy reserves, of 1.1 to 1.25 times the loan payment. To determine the debt coverage, lenders will want to examine current rent rolls, rental history reports, and income and expense statements from at least the previous two years. To say their research will be exhaustive is an understatement.

Here is what you need to know about commercial loans:

- For loan amounts under $1,000,000, commercial loans will most certainly be more difficult to obtain than residential loans.

- Loan fees and interest rates are generally significantly higher than for properties in the one- to four-unit range.

- Appraisals are more extensive and cost much more than residential appraisals.

- These types of loans usually take much longer to process than loans for residential properties.

## INTEREST RATES

Two types of interest rates are available on any kind of real estate loan: fixed and adjustable.

## FIXED-RATE MORTGAGES

Many investors prefer fixed-rate loans because they are predictable; you know exactly what you will be paying. If you get a fixed-rate loan at a good rate, all the more power to you. In the 2017 market, fixed rates were available on two-, three-, and four-unit buildings. On five units and up, one usually could find loans fixed for three to seven years, at which time they converted to adjustable loans. Nonetheless, when long-term interest rates are down, fixed-rate loans are highly sought after and should be considered.

## ADJUSTABLE-RATE MORTGAGES

An adjustable-rate loan is one where the interest rate and payment can change as the cost of money changes for the lender. The interest rate and payment may go up, or they may go down. What the rate will do actually depends on two factors: the current "index" and the current "margin." An index is generally based on US Treasury bill rates, US Treasury bond rates, or the cost of money in local federal districts. A margin is a bank's cost and profit. It varies depending on market conditions and competition. The margin is the lender's profit.

You can calculate the interest rate on an adjustable-rate mortgage (ARM) loan by using the following formula:

Current Rate of Index + Margin of Loan = Interest Rate

For example, if the index is .73 and the margin is 2.35, you can calculate the interest on an ARM as follows:

.73% Rate + 2.35% Margin = 3.08% Interest Rate

Most adjustable loans do not allow potential negative amortization. In guaranteeing that there will be no negative amortization, the lender builds in protection for potential interest-rate increases. To do that, most allow for two interest adjustments each year (one every six months). The maximum increase in the interest rate is usually 1 percent each period with a corresponding adjustment in the payment. For this maximum increase, the bank will absorb any increase above the 2 percent increase per year (or 1 percent every six months).

For the conservative investor who is working out a ten- to twenty-year retirement plan, the fixed-rate loan is probably best. That is, if the numbers work out so the property makes sense with the fixed rate. For many younger investors, the lower start rates on the adjustable loans may be the only way to buy. In that case, stick a bumper sticker on your car that says, "Adjustable-Rate Mortgage or Bust!" and go for it.

Regardless of the type of conventional loan you choose, it is important that you shop around for the best possible terms. Many variables will affect your costs. Use the following checklist to compare programs effectively:

- Interest rate

- Fixed or adjustable

- Loan-to-value ratio

- Debt coverage percentage

- Points

- Appraisal fee

- Environmental review fee

- Margin

- Index

- Interest rate cap

- Payment cap

- Required impounds

- Prepayment penalty

- Yield maintenance

- Recourse or nonrecourse

- Processing time

- Good-faith deposit

- Other fees

## ASSUMABLE LOANS

Assumable loans are ones already in place that can be assumed by the person purchasing the property. Rather than finding new financing and paying all the corresponding fees, assumable loans allow a buyer to pay a small fee—usually one point—and take over someone else's existing loan.

Assumable loans are great options because they often offer better terms than similar new loans. Perhaps interest rates were better at the time an original loan was put on the property. If so, a purchaser who takes over a loan like this would make out well. Additionally, after an assumable loan has been in place for many years, it starts paying off the principal at a rapid clip. For an investor preparing for retirement, an assumable loan makes sense because it may allow you to get a loan that will be paid off in full near the time you retire. There is nothing as comforting as starting retirement with a piece of income property that is paid off in full. Talk about cash flow!

## PRIVATE-PARTY FINANCING

The last source of real estate funding is through private-party financing. These loans are usually made by the sellers of the properties themselves wanting to take advantage of installment sales, and they offer several advantages over conventional loans. First of all, by obtaining private-party financing you can save a lot of money in lending fees because most of the costs associated with conventional financing do not apply to private loans. Second, because this is a private contract, the buyer and seller can create whatever win-win terms they want to make the deal work.

It may surprise you to learn that many sellers who offer private financing do not want any down payment at all. Instead of a big lump-sum down payment, which actually can be a tax headache for them, these sellers/financers are looking for monthly income from carrying the note as illustrated in chapter six on tax planning. Many of these sellers only want enough money down to pay the closing costs. After that, the income you will provide them is gravy.

So the rule is this: anything goes. A contract is like your own private set of laws, and the two parties to that contract can create whatever "laws" (terms) work for them. Many sellers may offer financing at lower interest rates than the going conventional rate and payment terms to fit most needs. In fact, it is not unusual for sellers to carry long-term financing with interest-only payments. Why? Because they make more money, that's why. Again, the situation becomes a win-win for everybody. In fact, we have seen many transactions in which the payments were lower than interest-only in order to wrap up the deal. Usually, it is because a seller has not kept the rents up with the market and thus a graduated payment schedule allows the buyer to raise rents over time.

The last thing to consider when looking at a private-party loan is the paid-in-full due date. As with a conventional loan, it can be one year, five years, or thirty years—whatever you agree on. You should not be surprised if the seller wants to set up some partial lump-sum payoffs at preset times. The seller may have loans he or she needs to pay off down the road or shell out the college tuition for a grandchild. In these situations, the seller should allow you to get the funds by refinancing the property and putting the private-party loan in the second position.

Another type of private lending is the "land sale contract" or "contract for deed." Here, the actual title to the property does not transfer at the time of the loan. Instead, the seller keeps the title in his or her name until the loan is paid off. Deals are often structured this way to help the buyer qualify. This is not unlike a car loan, where the lender keeps the title until the car is paid off in full.

One final source for private financing is known as the "hard-money market." Intended for the difficult-to-qualify buyer, hard-money loans are made by third parties at high interest rates. This may be due to the buyer's poor credit or because the property is in bad shape. Just know that hard-money loans are available for those deals that cannot get financed conventionally.

—— $ ——

"I found out about Buckingham Investment almost twenty years ago when I was looking for rental space for my property management company. Even though I am also a licensed real estate broker, an agent from Buckingham Investments has represented me numerous times because he simply 'gets it.' His knowledge of investment real estate combined with his market research gives an investor an upper hand at understanding market conditions and making the right decisions of when and how to invest. That direction and leadership leads to a long-term overall investment plan that will yield maximum returns for years to come, in any market."

—*Neil C.*

# —— CRITICAL CONCEPT ——

## He Who Has the Gold Makes the Rules

Many people talk about waiting until rates come down before they invest, and it costs them. When most of us buy, we need to borrow a large portion of the property cost. The main reason investors do this is for the benefits from the leverage. There is virtually nothing we can do to change the interest rates banks charge when we are ready to buy. You must forget what rates were six months or one year ago when it's time to buy. As long as the building you are looking at makes financial sense now with existing rates and fits your investment plan, BUY IT!

# 9

# Minding the Farm

*"Treat your customers like human beings—and they will
always come back."*

—L.L. Bean

The day you close escrow on a piece of property is the
day the hard work of being a real estate investor begins.
It's now time to take over managing your building and to
start running your new real estate business in earnest.

In this chapter, we offer some key lessons in property
management. My goal is to help you get a jump start on
taking over your building with total and complete confidence.

## BEFORE CLOSING

For years I recommended that clients manage their
first buildings themselves, so they gain that on-the-job
experience. As we all know the world has changed, and

despite all our labor-saving advances we seem to be busier than ever. So my new theme is "manage the manager." The reality is a professional property management company is a valuable asset to your team. They have years of experience and systems to make all the paperwork smooth. As you are working toward acquiring your first property, I recommend you begin looking for a management company. Your agent or friends who own property should be able to give you several referrals. Go meet with them, so you can find one with whom you feel comfortable. It will be helpful if you get this done *before* you find that first property. That way, you can get your management company to go along when you do your inspections because they will be able to give you valuable insight about the property you will ultimately turn over to them. This also will help because the day you close escrow you can turn everything over to them and they can take charge right away.

## OPEN FOR BUSINESS

Simplistic as it may sound, this really is a people business. Some real estate investors tend to focus on the money they're going to make and forget that you make the money by keeping the customer content. In this instance, the customer is your tenant. If you keep your tenants content, they will eventually reward you in kind. Namely, with their help, you will someday soon be able to retire in style.

When it comes to rental agreements, it would be wise not to use those preprinted ones that are available at your local stationery store. These all-purpose rental agreements are very general and lack the specific details necessary to protect you in case of a dispute. On the other hand, I do recommend you use rental agreements that you can obtain from your local apartment owners association. These agreements are usually written by lawyers who specialize in landlord/landlady-tenant law and will contain all the necessary standard clauses to protect both you and your tenants. Generally, your property management company will already have all the forms needed.

Should you go with month-to-month agreements or long-term leases? When you first take over the reins of control, the decision won't be up to you because you will be obligated to honor the previous agreements that you inherited. Once the terms of those agreements are met, however, the decision becomes all yours. You will find that local custom will often dictate what kinds of tenancies are standard in your area. In some communities, month-to-month agreements are preferred. In others, long-term leases are common. In short, month-to-month agreements allow landlords/landladies and tenants to terminate the agreement with just thirty to sixty days notice. Leases, on the other hand, lock both parties in at an agreed-on rental rate for an extended period of time (usually one year for residential income property). Therefore, the type of tenancies that you choose will ultimately depend on the amount of flexibility you desire.

Finally, you should provide an interior inspection checklist for review by the tenant and you or your property manager. On taking ownership, walk the unit with your tenant and go over the following checklist together. When finished, make sure you both sign and date it. This will eliminate most disagreements over deposit refunds in the event you need to charge them because of any material damage they did to the unit.

When you are taking over a building with existing tenants, you probably will not be able to do this. If there are major problems, you should discover them during your inspection and get them corrected prior to closing escrow.

Interior Inspection Checklist

- Condition of carpet

- Condition of vinyl and other floor coverings

- Condition of paint

- Holes in walls

- Condition of ceiling

- List of owner's appliances and their condition

- Condition of doors, windows, and window screens

- Condition of garage, carport, and/or storage area

- List of keys and accessories

- Anything else you can think of

Protecting your privacy should be of paramount importance to you. Here are a few things you can do to ensure your privacy:

- Never give out your home address to your tenants or your resident manager.

- Never give out your home phone number to your tenants.

- Have your home phone number unlisted.

- Get the caller ID feature added to your phone service.

- Set up a post office box before you buy any piece of property. This way, your address will not show up on any utility bills or public documents.

Now that you're in business for yourself, you'll also need a policy about accepting personal checks for rent payment. Most management companies will already have one in place. In many cases, they may now also be set up for direct deposit.

## HUD HOUSING

Because many people cannot afford adequate housing, the government has created several assistance programs. The most common is through the Department of Housing and Urban Development. HUD's original goal dates back to the Housing Act of 1949. The purpose of this law was to provide "a decent home and a suitable living environment for every American family."

The program under which this rental-payment assistance is administered is called "Section 8." Some cities receive Section 8 assistance, and others maintain offices that administer housing assistance programs via vouchers. If qualified for either of these programs, the applicants will have part of their rent paid by the government, while they will be responsible for the balance. In most cases, the tenant's share of the rent does not exceed 20 percent to 30 percent of his or her monthly income. The advantage of having Section 8 or voucher tenants is it makes decent homes affordable to a larger section of the population. What's more, the majority of their rent is paid for by the government and, thankfully, Uncle Sam almost always pays on time.

Part of the job of HUD is to ascertain the general market rent for various size apartments and houses in the community. This schedule becomes the top rent tenants are able to pay, including any subsidies by HUD. What's beneficial is if you have properties in an area with HUD subsidies, you may find the rent HUD sets to be more than reasonable. These rates are based on the size of the unit, utilities paid, appliances provided, condition of the neighborhood, and so on.

One hurdle you will need to face with a HUD-assisted tenant is the inspection of your property by a HUD official. HUD's goal is to provide decent, safe, and sanitary conditions for the tenants. As long as the apartment passes the yearly HUD inspection, it will meet the program's requirements. If so, as a landlord/landlady, you could benefit for years to come with rental rates at or above the top of the market.

## DISCRIMINATION

Regardless of whether you are the resident-manager of a fifty-unit apartment complex or the owner of a few modest two- and three-unit buildings, federal antidiscrimination laws now apply to you, as may a number of state and local ordinances. The federal Civil Rights Act and Fair Housing Act prohibit owners from discriminating on the basis of race, ethnic background, national origin, religion, and sex. The Americans with Disabilities Act (ADA) effectively prohibits discrimination against someone with a disability.

When it comes to picking new tenants, the law says that if you are faced with two equally qualified tenants, it is okay to pick one over another for no other reason than you liked one better. There is nothing discriminatory in that. If, however, you have a pattern of not choosing women, African Americans, Jews, or other "minorities," you leave yourself open to what could be an expensive lawsuit.

Even if you are not discriminating when renting your units, you should be just as concerned with the *appearance* of discrimination. For example, your apartment building may be occupied only by young, white urban professionals. In this instance, you appear to be discriminating even if you are not.

The key to minimizing this risk is to set up some objective, legitimate business criteria when looking for new tenants and adhere to it. The law says you must treat all applicants equally, so use the same criteria in every case. Look consistently for such things as three personal references, a steady employment history, and good credit. In fact, as part of your requirements for tenancy, you should decide upon a minimum FICO score.

Most management companies have policies for this issue, so be sure to discuss it with them.

## UTILITIES AND INSURANCE

During escrow, you should have found out the local utility companies and who does the regular maintenance work on your building. Now that you are the new owner, you will have to transfer all these services to your name. The local utility companies also might want deposits or run credit checks for your new services. Make sure you handle these issues well in advance of closing. It would make a poor first impression on your tenants if the utilities were shut off the very day you took over.

When it comes to insurance, you were probably required by the lender to purchase some for your building before you ever closed escrow. This insurance covered you and the lender in case of fire. But what about insurance for the manager and the workers who come on to the property to work? Getting some insurance to cover them might be a wise idea as well. You may not think you have any employees for your modest triplex, but perhaps you do: the kid who cuts your grass, the plumber who fixes the leaky faucets in the bathrooms, and the tenant who shows the vacant unit for you will all probably be considered employees by a court of law if they get injured while working on your property. Thus, you should find out if your existing policy covers these casual workers. If not, you need to get a policy to cover them.

One way around having to buy another pricey insurance policy would be to use contractors who can prove they have their own workers' compensation insurance before they do any work for you. Self-insured contractors, however, usually charge much more than the casual local handyperson does, because these contractors have to pay all their own fees and obtain all the licenses for the work they do.

## APARTMENT OWNERS ASSOCIATION

Now that you're a landlord/landlady, you should join the local apartment owners association. You can locate one easily enough by searching through the National Apartment Association offices by state (www.naahq.org), looking in the Yellow Pages, or by contacting your state department of real estate. If for some reason there isn't one in your own community, try to find an apartment owners association in the nearest major city and join that group.

Why is an apartment owners association important to join? These organizations are usually run by experienced apartment owners and professional property managers. Their purpose is to help other owners and managers. Most provide excellent classes and monthly newsletters, which will keep you up-to-date on current events, local laws and relevant ordinances, rental rates, and any changes taking place in the market. They also carry advertisements for plumbers, roofers, electricians, and other service providers who can help you when you need it. In addition, many associations will supply you with various forms you might need, including rental agreements. Some even are able to run credit checks on any potential new tenants you may have.

I suggest you join, even though you are using a property management company.

## WHO'S DOING WHAT?

It's important for you to stay current on what's happening in your neighborhood. You probably did some initial investigation before you bought the property, but now you need to keep an ongoing log about the neighborhood and the buildings that surround yours. Some of the things to note in your landlord's/landlady's notebook would include:

- Number of units in the surrounding buildings
- Number of properties on the streets
- Phone numbers and/or email addresses from the For Rent signs
- Amenities in the other properties
- Rental rates and terms on the vacancies
- Overall condition of the streets
- Location and phone numbers of local police and fire departments

This isn't a project that you should begin and finish in one day. Rather, it will be an ongoing process for as long as you are building your nest egg through real estate. And because this is a working notebook, it doesn't have to be fancy. You want to use it to keep track of the facts you learn about the streets and buildings that surround your property. The primary goal of your notes is to get a broad overview of what's happening at all times, which will help you make decisions about your property in the future.

This is something you should do even though you have a management company. This falls under the category of managing your manager.

## DETERMINING VACANCY RATES

You'll notice that the first item on the preceding list is to find out how many units are in the surrounding buildings. By knowing how many units are out there, you can determine the neighborhood's vacancy rate and thus be able to monitor changes in vacancy trends.

There is a fast and easy way to determine the local vacancy rate. To begin with, just count the number of mailboxes that you see in the neighborhood. It is not necessary that you be 100 percent accurate because you want just an estimate of how many units there are. Once you know the number, you can figure out the vacancy rate by counting the number of For Rent signs or looking at online listings in the same area and then divide that number by the number of mailboxes. The math will look like this:

$$\text{Number of For Rent Signs} \div \text{Number of Mailboxes} = \text{Vacancy Rate}$$

This method of determining the vacancy rate is an inexact science, but it should help you determine a general vacancy rate at a given time. With this knowledge at your fingertips, you always will be able to stay one step ahead of the competition.

## DETERMINING RENTAL RATES

It is easy to do a rent survey. One good way is to pretend you are a prospective tenant. Whenever you see a For Rent sign in your neighborhood, jot down the phone number and call. Make sure you ask all the applicable questions of a prospective tenant and record the details. You can also review online listings to get most of the same information.

Rental Survey Questions

- How much is the unit renting for?

- How many bedrooms and bathrooms does the unit have?

- What is the square footage of the apartment?

- What amenities are included?

- Do they accept pets?

- Will it be a month-to-month agreement or a long-term lease?

- How much will it cost to move in?

- Can you see the inside of the unit?

By habitually doing this exercise, you will accumulate plenty of ammunition to guard yourself against a complacent management company. It is easy for a management company to produce good numbers if it never pushes the rents to the upper end of the market. But this is a business, and your cash-on-cash return and nest egg depend on management keeping the rental rate at the correct level. Your tenants will never moan if your rents are too low. In fact, they'll be thrilled and probably will never move. But keep in mind that when it comes time to refinance or sell, any lower-than-market rental rates will directly affect the value of your building.

## FILLING A VACANCY

The key to getting your apartment filled as quickly as possible lies in doing the right kind of advertising for your soon-to-be-vacant unit. Some of the best advertising methods are:

- list with online rental services like Craigslist;

- place a rental sign or banner out front;

- offer a referral fee to an existing tenant;

- hold open houses on weekends;

- post flyers at local businesses;

- place ads in local newspapers;

- send direct-mail material to tenants in similar buildings; and

- register with rental agencies.

Your decision on how much or how little advertising you will need to do will be based on the results of your ongoing vacancy surveys. Normally, the lower the vacancy rate, the quicker the unit will fill and the less effort is needed. Most important is you get the apartment occupied, so you don't lose any rent. No doubt your management company will have a policy on handling turnovers. You should discuss that, so you have a clear understanding.

## A POLICY ON PETS

When you buy your building, you will inherit a pet policy from the previous owner. Now that the building is under your watch, should you consider renting your units to tenants with pets? Don't say *no* so fast. Here are some reasons we say *yes* to pets:

- You can command a premium rent from someone with a pet.

- Because most landlords/landladies don't allow pets, it's difficult for someone with a pet to find a new residence. By considering these tenants, you will have a large pool of grateful tenants to pick from.

- Because it's difficult for pet owners to find an apartment that allows pets, pet owners generally stay in the apartment longer than nonpet owners do.

- Most pet owners will be willing to put down a large security deposit if you accept them as a tenant. If the pet damages the apartment, you will have the money to fix it and make it as good as new for the next tenant.

- Accepting tenants with pets is a good method of combating periods of high vacancy.

As you can see, there are plenty of good reasons why you may want to accept tenants with pets—all of them financial. If you do decide to consider pets, you should advertise your unit that way: "Will consider small pets. Call to discuss." In most cases your management company will already have a policy on this issue.

## HAPPY TENANTS

This chapter began with a quote from L. L. Bean talking about the importance of keeping your customers happy. Your customers are your tenants, and making sure they get their money's worth for the dollars they pay in rent is a key component to your ultimate success. This is the basic philosophy most businesses operate under, but when it comes to renting apartments, this sometimes becomes easy to forget.

Lots of investors buy a building or two, fix them up, and fill them with nice new tenants. Unfortunately, as the years go on, they often let their buildings deteriorate. But this doesn't have to happen. If you want to have a sharp building with a great tenant base, fix it up, manage it properly, and maintain the property at all times. This will ensure two things:

1.  The current tenants will want to stay in the nice home you helped create for them.

2.  Prospective tenants will see how you care for the building and will be willing to pay you top dollar to live there.

Remember that most restaurant customers don't complain about bad food; they just don't come back. With units, if you let the building deteriorate without keeping it up, the tenants will just find another place to live rather than complain to a deaf ear.

It's important to take care of tenant requests as fast as possible. The truth is most people don't like to complain. So when they do, assume the problem has been going on long enough that it is really starting to be a nuisance. You also should get in the habit of asking your tenants how things are going in the building whenever you see them. They may forget to mention that little leak under their sink unless you ask. On the other hand, by finding out about small problems early on, you can nip bigger problems in the bud. The end result will always be more money in your pocket.

## RAISING THE RENT

Raising rents is always a sensitive issue with owners and tenants alike. The bottom line is this is a business, and your cash-on-cash return and your building's ultimate value depend on your rental rate. Therefore, raising rents periodically is part of the deal. Your tenants know it, and now so do you.

The first secret to raising rents successfully is to know what other owners in your neighborhood are getting for comparable units. If they are getting more than you are, then an increase is probably in order. Many landlords/landladies fear that their tenants will move out if they raise the rents. The truth, however, is most people won't go to the trouble and expense of moving. In a worst-case scenario, your tenant may give you notice and move out. In that instance, get the apartment ready as soon as possible and charge the next tenant the market rent you deserve.

To soften the blow of an increase, consider doing something extra for your tenants. It doesn't hurt to follow or precede a cost-of-living increase with some upgrades to the building. You might consider putting some plants or flowers in front of the building or new doormats in front of the apartments. Another idea would be to have all the outside windows washed at your expense. Even a $15 gift certificate to the local coffee shop would remind them how lucky they are to have you as their landlord/landlady.

One way to get the message out to your tenants about rents in an increasing market is to prominently display the current rate on your For Rent signs or in online listings. When they see your other units being rented at a much higher rate, they will be far less apt to object when they get a raise, especially if they are paying less than market rent.

"Finding Buckingham Investments changed my life. I met Marty Stone, the broker for Buckingham Investments, fourteen years ago, and he sat down and showed me why investing in real estate was the key to long-term financial security. Over the last fourteen years, I have located excellent investment opportunities in real estate working with a team of owners, investors, and other real estate professionals to find properties, to locate properties before they hit the market, and to find their clients the best properties to invest in. I have met my goals of creating passive income from my properties."

—*Mark O.*

—— CRITICAL CONCEPT ——

## Mixing People and Profit

Property management is a people business with more customer issues than most industries. This is because you are selling (renting) a commodity that is somebody's home. This can create more emotional issues for you (the owner) and your customer (the tenant). For that reason, hiring a professional management company to handle the day-to-day affairs works best for most investors.

# 10

# Putting It All Together

*"Dare to live the life you have dreamed for yourself.*
*Go forward and make your dreams come true."*

—Ralph Waldo Emerson

We've covered a lot of information in this book. My hope is you have been moved enough by my message so that you will take a positive step to find a better way to fund your future.

A mentor of mine has always preached, "If you always do what you've always done, you'll always get what you always got." Truer words couldn't be spoken, especially for the 95 percent of American retirees who retire practically broke. To add insult to injury, the amount of money needed to retire comfortably is increasing and the effects of inflation often hit retirees the hardest. The good news is that medical advances are giving all of us the possibility of many more years of a healthy life after retirement. The question is "If you're practically broke when you do retire, is that really good news?"

Most of us probably never gave it much thought when we started our careers, but work is something we'll be doing for thirty to forty years of our lives. While working, we honorably and consistently pay into Social Security or maybe even a company pension plan, all with the expectation that these investments will pay off as they are supposed to. As the future of Social Security grows ever dimmer, however, and the financial setbacks and losses of the last recession reverberate, it's clear that to think we'll be taken care of in retirement by others is nothing but a pipe dream.

To solve this dilemma, I haven't suggested any major life-changing moves. Instead, one solution is not to fall for the Social Security/401(k)/pension fund hocus-pocus trap. There's no way these things will fill the bill when your time comes. Another solution is to refuse to abdicate the responsibility for your retirement by turning it over to experts picked by the people who are "supposed to know." If they really knew, the 95 percent statistic wouldn't be what it is.

No, you need to take charge of this most important issue and make concrete plans now to create a worthwhile nest egg later. I say do it via real estate or any other way that works. But, above all, just do it so you don't have to work forever. Of course, you know that I believe real estate is the best and safest way. My challenge has been to lay out the facts so that you believe it too. The limited space in this book has allowed us to touch only the high points of investing in real estate. This review should have given you an outline of the topics that need additional study and research.

I encourage you to use the three-part system I laid out earlier. Remember, I'm talking about a process that will pay off in fifteen to thirty years. I want you to get started but, as important, get started on the right foot. To recap, the components of the system are:

1. **Learn** about real estate as an investment and your local market.

2. **Plan** how to reach your goals.

3. **Invest** in property that will help you reach your goals.

I realize how hard it will be for you to get started. There are always people around who will tell you why it won't work. They will fill you with fear about property management and recount how their uncle or friend lost everything trying to do just what you're contemplating pursuing. But these are the people who will be in that 95 percent practically broke group. That is, unless they hit the lottery, which, of course, they play every week. What I hope you have learned is that I'm not talking about winning by chance, like the lottery. I'm talking about investing based on education—your education.

My thought process in this book has been to present an ultraconservative approach to this topic—that is, buy a property or two with the goal of getting them paid off by the time you retire. This simple plan should make a significant difference in the quality of your retirement. What makes this logic tough to sell is it takes fifteen to thirty years to see the real payoff. On the other hand, it's a lot easier to motivate people with dreams of get-rich-quick—like "placing tiny little ads in papers" to sell things or buying and flipping distressed real estate for nothing down. Sure, these ideas work sometimes, but more often than not people flock to them too quickly and the inherent pitfalls swallow them whole.

Odds are if you accept your probable fate, you are on the road to a better way to care for you and your family. No doubt that a modest investment in real estate now could allow you to have the fruitful future you have dreamed of. For many, getting started small will lead to greater investments and bigger rewards beyond their wildest expectations. But let's not get ahead of ourselves. Never forget that the number one goal is to provide financial security for your retirement. Anything beyond that is gravy.

You'll remember that I began each chapter with a quote. Some were famous; some were catchy; some poignant; some funny; some not. As we get older, we learn what's behind people saying such things: it's usually because their words convey a hard-earned truth. In most cases, it's easier to make a change when you personally experience the truth. The truth of the topic of our book—retirement—isn't as forgiving.

I have a framed print in the lobby of my office. Below a silhouette of a golfer making a perfect back swing, the print reads, "In the game of life, play well. You don't get a second round." It's an interesting saying to put under a golfer because there is such a thing as a "mulligan." A mulligan is a friendly unwritten rule that allows a player to retake a stroke with no penalty. The idea is the golfer will have a better shot the next time he or she swings the club.

Because you don't get a mulligan in the game of life, all I ask is that you take my message seriously and do it differently than the rest of the 95 percent. Play your retirement well!

# Glossary

ACCOMMODATOR   A neutral third party that assists in completing a delayed 1031 tax-deferred exchange. The accommodator is usually a corporate entity.

ACTIVE INVESTOR   An IRS classification for a real estate investor who materially participates in running a property.

ADJUSTABLE-RATE MORTGAGE (ARM)   A loan in which the future interest rate may change, with that change determined by an index of rates. The frequency and amount of change are limited by the mortgage contract.

ADJUSTED COST BASIS   For the purpose of computing capital gains or losses, the adjusted cost basis is the original purchase price plus closing costs, plus the cost value of improvements done while the property was held, less all depreciation claimed.

ADJUSTED GROSS INCOME   The income from a piece of property after any adjustments are made for other income or rental losses.

**ADJUSTED SALES PRICE**   The price of a property after deducting the costs of sale.

**APPRAISAL**   The process of estimating the current market value of a property.

**APPRECIATION**   Increase in value due to any cause.

**AMORTIZATION**   The repayment terms of a loan, including the required principal and interest, based on the interest rate and the period of time allowed to pay down or amortize the loan to zero.

**ANNUAL DEPRECIATION ALLOWANCE**   The deduction one can take on one's income tax against earnings to recapture the cost of the structures on one's property.

**ANNUAL EXPENSES**   All the costs that one must pay to operate one's property.

**AVERAGE RETURN ON EQUITY (AROE)**   Each year that one owns a property, one can calculate the return on the equity for that year. Add up the returns for several years and divide by the number of years to get the average.

**BASIS**   The cost of the building on one's property, plus improvements and fixtures, which can be depreciated but not claimed as deductions. Basis is calculated as original cost plus capital improvements, less depreciation.

**BOOT**   An IRS term for taxable proceeds from a sale other than cash.

**CAP**   A limit on the amount of increase a lender may impose under the terms of an adjustable-rate mortgage. The annual cap specifies the maximum annual increase, and the lifetime cap specifies the overall increase the lender is allowed to pass on to the borrower.

CAPITAL EXPENSE   The outlay to purchase any asset with a useful life of over one year. The tax treatment for such expenditure allows the asset to be "capitalized," which means the cost is deducted over its useful life, according to the applicable depreciation method, rather than as an expense in the current period.

CAPITAL GAINS   The profits one makes on investments.

CAPITALIZATION OF INCOME   A valuation method achieved by dividing the net income of a property by the capitalization rate of that kind of property.

CAPITALIZATION RATE   The percentage return that one gets by dividing the net income from a property by the price of the property.

CASH FLOW   The amount of money received from rental income each month, less the amount paid out in mortgage payments, the purchase of capital assets, and payment of any operating expenses. Cash flow is not the same as profit, because it includes nondeductible payments.

CASH-ON-CASH RETURN   The cash profit from an investment divided by the cash invested to buy the investment.

COLLECTED RENT   Amount of rental income actually collected.

COMMERCIAL LOANS   Any loan not classified as a residential loan, usually on five units or more.

COMMERCIAL PROPERTY   Nonresidential property operated for business use.

COMPARABLES (COMPS)   Properties that are similar to the property being considered or appraised.

COMPARATIVE ANALYSIS    A method of appraisal in which selling prices of similar properties are used as the basis for arriving at the value estimate. It also is known as the market data approach.

COMPOUND INTEREST    Interest paid on original principal and on the accrued interest.

COMPOUND INTEREST ALGORITHM    A mathematical formula used to calculate the percentage return when profits from an investment are reinvested over a given period of time.

COST BASIS    One's basis for calculating the capital gain on a property one owns.

DEBT COVERAGE    The comparison between the net income of a property and the loan payments on the property.

DELAYED EXCHANGE    An IRS-approved technique for completing an exchange of equity to postpone taxes. Also called a "Starker" exchange.

DEMAND APPRECIATION    Appreciation in value related to an increase in the desire to possess the property.

DEPARTMENT OF VETERANS AFFAIRS    Also known as the VA, it is the federal government agency that administers GI or VA loans. Previously known as the Veterans Administration.

DEPRECIABLE IMPROVEMENTS    The value of the structures on a property that the IRS allows one to depreciate.

DEPRECIATED VALUE    The value that remains after deducting the depreciation from the cost base for a property.

DEPRECIATION    Loss of value due to any cause, as an appraisal term.

DEPRECIATION ALLOWANCE   The dollar amount the IRS allows one to deduct each year from the earnings from a property.

EQUITY   The portion of real estate one owns. In the case of a property bought for $200,000 with a $133,000 mortgage, the equity is the difference ($67,000).

EQUITY GROWTH FROM APPRECIATION   The increase in a property's value because of the effects of inflation.

EQUITY GROWTH FROM LOAN REDUCTION   The increase in the owner's equity in a property from the payoff of the financing.

FEDERAL HOUSING ADMINISTRATION (FHA)   An agency created by the National Housing Act of 1934 to provide a home-financing system through federal mortgage insurance.

FIXED EXPENSES   The regular recurring costs required in holding a property, such as taxes and insurance.

FIXED-RATE LOAN   A loan in which the interest rate will not change during the contract period.

FULLY AMORTIZED   Refers to a loan that is completely paid off when all the payments are made.

GI LOAN   Also called a VA loan, it is available to veterans under a federal government program administered by the Department of Veterans Affairs.

GROSS RENT MULTIPLIER   A factor used for appraising income-producing property. The multiplier times the gross income gives an approximate property value.

**HIGHEST AND BEST USE**   The use of property for the most profitable, efficient, and appropriate purpose, given the zoning and other restrictions placed on the land.

**IMPROVEMENTS**   Any structure or addition to a piece of raw land.

**INFLATION**   An economic condition occurring when the money supply increases in relation to goods and associated with rising wages and costs and decreasing purchasing power.

**INFLATIONARY APPRECIATION**   Refers to the value of a product increasing due to inflation taking place in the economy.

**INSTALLMENT NOTE**   The name of the note carried by a seller of a property, which gives the seller special tax benefits.

**INSTALLMENT SALE**   The sale of a property where the seller carries an installment note.

**INVEST**   To commit money or capital in business in order to earn a financial return; the outlay of money for income or profit.

**LAND SALES CONTRACT**   Another name for a conditional sales contract. The buyer takes possession, and the seller retains title until all conditions are met.

**LEVERAGE**   The use of borrowed money to purchase an investment that realizes enough income to cover the expense of the financing, with the excess accruing to the purchaser.

**MARGIN**   The number that is added to the index of a loan to get the final interest rate of the loan.

**MORTGAGE**   A contract that makes a specific property the security for payment of a debt.

NEG-AM LOANS   Loans where you have the option to pay a lower payment than is needed to pay all the interest due.

NEGATIVE AMORTIZATION   Occurs when the payments on an adjustable loan are not sufficient to pay all the interest due. In this case, the loan increases by the amount of the unpaid interest.

NO-NEG LOANS   Loans where the payment will always pay all the interest due on the loan.

OPERATING EXPENSES   Periodic expenditures necessary to maintain the property and continue the production of effective gross income.

PASSIVE INVESTORS   An IRS term that refers to someone who is limited in the deductions that can be claimed against earnings.

POINT   One percent of the loan amount; an additional charge added on by a lender as a fee assessed for getting the loan. Points are also called "loan fees."

POSITIVE CASH FLOW   A situation in which cash receipts are greater than cash payments.

RENT SURVEY   A survey done to find out what other owners are charging for rent in a given area.

RESPA   Real Estate Settlement Procedures Act, a federal law that ensures buyers and sellers in certain federally related residential real estate transactions receive full disclosure of all settlement costs, so they can shop around for settlement services.

RETURN ON EQUITY (ROE)   A percentage of return calculated by dividing annual net income by equity.

RETURN ON INVESTMENT (ROI)    Interest or profit from an investment.

SCHEDULED RENT    The current rent scheduled for all the units in a building.

SECTION 8    The federal government's principal medium for housing assistance, authorized by the Housing and Community Development Act of 1974, which provides for new construction and rehabilitation.

STARKER EXCHANGE    A type of tax-deferred exchange that got its name from the court case of the same name. Also called a "delayed" exchange.

STRAIGHT NOTE    A note in which the amount of the loan and the interest are paid with only one payment.

TAX BENEFITS    The tax savings from property ownership.

TAX-DEFERRED EXCHANGE (1031 TAX-DEFERRED EXCHANGE)    A method of deferring capital gains by exchanging real property for other like-kind property.

TAX SHELTER    An investment with paper losses that can be used to lower one's otherwise taxable income. In other words, the tax loss from the tax-shelter investment is a write-off against regular salary or other income and therefore "shelters" that income.

THREE-PARTY EXCHANGE    A tax-deferred exchange that involves three different parties.

TURNOVER    When one tenant moves out of a property and another moves in; usually means no loss of rent.

UP-LEG PROPERTY    The larger property in a tax-deferred exchange.

US DEPARTMENT OF HOUSING AND URBAN DEVELOPMENT (HUD) A government agency established in 1965 that provides federal assistance in planning, developing, and managing public housing.

USEFUL LIFE   For tax purposes, this is the period of time over which one must depreciate a property. As a general concept, this is the period of time a property is expected to be functional.

VACANCY RATE   The average percentage of units that are vacant in a given market area.

VALUE APPRECIATION   The increase in value of a property from all causes.

VARIABLE EXPENSES   Expenses on a property that tend to be different each month or pay period.

VETERANS ADMINISTRATION (VA) A government agency that is set up to help individuals who have served in the armed forces; now part of the Department of Veterans Affairs.

# About the Author

M artin Stone is the founder/co-owner of Buckingham Investments and has a degree in finance from the University of Southern California. He has been a successful real estate broker and investor for forty-plus years, building more than fifty multifamily apartment buildings, commercial properties, and single-family homes and managing over one thousand units, and has written and lectured extensively about all areas related to property. He lives in El Segundo, California, with his wife of thirty-three years, Lori, a cancer survivor. They enjoy traveling with their sons and grandchildren, as well as volunteering for the Avon Breast Cancer Walk.